My First Book

I self-published my first book in 2024, *2intone dot us*, and I will put background from it into this book. Any indented text here, will be coming from the book *2intone dot us,* (second edition, 7x10 inch hardcover and ISBN: 9798340869579), referenced as (*) (Mandell, October 30, 2024). I tried to not have many other references than my first printed book.

I believe that my +Meself+ is a reference with my first book and in this book here too. So I will include some quotes from my first book here to consciously describe how I do reverse speech. I call my version of doing +reverse speech+ as Subresonate Voice, (SV). I listened to the SV, after reading the words here as a Conscious Voice, (CV), and if I found a message from my +Meself+ in this text then I will show that this was coming from SV, this text and my +Meself+ by putting my +Meself's+ words in underlined, **bold** and ~tildes.~ This analysis from CV to SV shows a faith that the subconscious is real and my +Meself+ is willing to help me.

So in this book I will identify comments from my higher self or +Meself+ as bold, underline text with tilde, as a type of subconscious quotation mark. I want to give respect to where it is due as I believe that my +Meself+ is real. If I don't know where the message is from then I will not have an underlining of the SV. If I SV this text and find that the CV is relevant then I will underline this text and give my SV after it, with a note. This is my faith. I don't want to suffer from the subconscious and not be deep in understanding with stepping stones to wisdom.

Some abbreviations are: Objective to Subjective Analysis (OSA). OSA is a way to think of a problem's solution through a story. Another abbreviation is Stimulated Back Track Mechanics (SBTM). SBTM is listening to someone, do a recording on your own memory of the conversation, then listen to the SV, this avoids the +liquid-de+ problem with BTM. Also, below I reference the Real Three Dimensions and Time (R3DT), which is what I call on our Earth, objective and show me the facts with science.

My Second Book

I was looking to add to *How to Trade ES-Futures*, because I needed to put an adject or additional updates as to what happened to my trading and how I'm going to make it better (Mandell, November 12, 2024). I also want to attempt to try to get this second edition of my second book accepted into the Barnes & Noble computer system so that I can promote it in their stores. So here I put a copyright on this edition, as this might help for me to be promoting this book, not just for the royalties.

My Dad's Trading

My Dad traded at the Minneapolis Grain Exchange in Minneapolis, Minnesota, starting September 30, 1986, according to his account application with the A.S. Polonyi Co., and I remember him having floor badge number 770. I have a broker trading card and it is included on pages 114 and 118. I went to the Commodity Futures Exchange Commission website to see information about Polonyi and it was out from being a Futures Commission Merchant on March 25, 1992. I think my Dad left the Minneapolis Grain Exchange, after 1992.

I dedicate this edition to my Dad's futures trading, as this book is published for his fourth year of being passed away or April 17, 2026.

About the Author

Hello, I'm Matt Mandell and I wanted to produce this book because I wanted to sell my first book at Barnes & Noble, but could not get it into their computer system. I SV Monday through Saturday at about 11 a.m. which gives me one day, sunset to sunset, to relax from the subconscious and praise God, over each weekend. SV, as our internal voice, this can open up information that is subconscious and can be revealed to us consciously. I tried to use SV to help me trade.

When I traded S&P 500 futures, symbol ES, I would use SV to try to decode the market. To my detriment I lost my money in the market, now I feel I can do it the right way, if I take my time, no heart pounding, then outcomes will be better.

I will try again and when I get enough money to use, I will refund my trading account. In the meantime, I'm uncovering the way I need to trade and hammer these nails into a coffin so I don't loose money again in ES, just make it back.

I will go into detail on how I should think about trading ES-futures and come up with important rules to keep me, okay. I don't want to go off into some crazy tantrum and trade into madness, losing money, but have wisdom and form an understanding. My personal website for the subconscious is at: https://2intone.us which has this book for sale on the home page.

Introduction

You can witness water making a level. Water can be a metaphor for the unconscious to the subconscious, in that water is acting as a thinking pattern in the mind that cannot be seen, it is in higher dimensions. Pour water from the unconscious into something and the water will go into every crevice to make a level. One can think of a solution to a problem by immersing into every area of concern or question associated to the problem. The water level formed is the truth because of gravity. By the gravitational laws of the universe a level is formed with water on a planet. It is wise to speak words to help others, as truthful words describe wisdom. Words are as water, in that words can form a level.

Words are our power, as human beings. We can speak to it and it is so because we use wisdom from experience of doing something, over and over again. In order to use your thoughts you have to think first. Words can help others realize their value by listening to SV, because they will be connecting subconscious words to thoughts, as water. When people listen to your words they can comprehend them well.

With the spirit of water, people may sink into your conversation, because they had similar thoughts, but were not able to put them into their words. We as humans can help each other out by exposing our thoughts with: words, to save a soul; feelings, to show love; or setting others onto the right track in life with a spirit. So I’m taking the objective, thoughtful actions and combining them into the spirit as a water or a +liquid-de+ experience with my +Meself+ to help me trade, because I do SV.

Having a subconscious dossier on your +meself+ can help yourself to know the ES-futures market with your intuition. Trading ES-futures is also objective because you click buy or sell, but is also subjective as the market needs to find the buyers and sellers, as in with the open outcry in the old pit at the Chicago Mercantile Exchange (CME).

The trading pit was just steps

into the floor where, I think, the market makers would stand to see the signals from the buyers and sellers along and around the higher steps up to floor level. This trade involved risk as money was changing hands with hand signals and yells.

The objective part is the risking of money to try to make more money because the market finds buyers and sellers, all matched-up. However, things could go wrong for some as money in the brokerage account could be all gone, that is why it is called risk money. The mind is subjective and that makes some of the trades subjective by the human mind. If one can enter the thoughts of the market and see the courses or choices available and get a sense of the general market direction then money can be acquired in the S&P 500 Futures market.

This book relates trading S&P 500 Futures, code named, ES-futures, with the subconscious and using SV. ES-futures are contracts for a future price of the S&P 500 group of companies that span a set of three months into the future where the futures contract will then expire or be delivered. I would never trade the futures contract that was expiring, just look at the volume. The safest trade instrument is the most current on the list and has the most volume traded. You can trade an ES-futures' lot during the day and then sell it to get a profit, up to 45 minutes after the closing bell.

I'm going to attempt to convince

you that you can make money doing this as I'm going to be making money with this method in the near future. I will be following rules and not deviate, by keeping the emotions in check. As I type this book into my computer for you all to read, know and understand with the help from God.

I believe God did communicate to me (through my +Meself+) that I should only trade ES-futures once a trading session. A trading session for ES-futures is being basically on a weekday from 5:00 p.m. to 3:45 p.m. Central Time, the next business day. The one trading should be aware that ES-futures has a lot of leverage and can move quickly and theoretically even with a stop, can lose money. The market could jump over a stop and that would be a catastrophe for someone on the wrong side of the trade.

I think God is important, especially if you have faith in the spirit world or above the R3DT. Some may say, you need to go to a shrink to make your mind smaller or get a new mind on things and think differently with your brain. However, the problem this person is trying to shrink smaller might not be the problem. The problem may be in fact, that the connection to God is faulty or intermittent. Kinda like an intermittent wall outlet that trips a fuse when an appliance is running. This is because this appliance is just fine, but the connection to the power is arcing and tripping the main fuse in the fuse box, it needs a new tight connection installed in or on the wall, not a new appliance. So in turn, the psychic forces are not proving I have a bad brain, I just need a solid connection to God that lets the power flow unimpeded, my brain works fine.

The market will flow like water and when there is a barrier it will find a way to get around it because the market has power. I can make money in the market, so I just need to find this flow, psychic moving information. So center yourselves and see the flow with your third eye because the market is going to flow with or without you. You might as will be with the market, be part of the discovery of where it goes and be at one with that old pit in the CME. If you can make a trade then yell and step in and get into the market, because the market can make money and wants to hold wealth. The wealth goes up, just as inflation goes up.

I will use the term "points," for what I've heard described as how much the market went up or down. In the ES-futures market, a one point move will add or subtract $50 from your futures trading platform with one mini lot in a trade. There are four ticks to a point so each tick with one lot traded would then move $12.50, with the leverage of the trade equal to $50 times the number of points that the ES-futures market is currently traded at all divided by the risk in your futures account controlling that one-lot trade. That is a lot of leverage. Say the ES-futures market is at 7000 points and you have $7000 in your account, with an

ES-mini, then that is a 50:1 leverage. Now there are patterns that the market takes if you have patience to watch and learn from them as the market turns and moves, so one can make money on this speculation of the market.

Let's start with $5000 and wire the money to your trusted futures broker that you did some research on. Next, we need to know how to use the trading platform to buy or sell an ES-future's trading lot. I trade with just one lot. I only trade once per day because of what other people say and what my +Meself+ warns me of: **~Matt if you trade more than one lot a day I see you as penny less, and I don't want to see that.~** By definition, one lot controls $50 times the current market point amount, on the chart. So this means ES is leveraged and an ES-futures account containing risk capital, my risk capital will be $5000, can control this one lot amount during a trade. If we have no stops we could loose money and the only thing to stop it would be your futures broker, if your account gets to about $400 to $800 dollars left in it. Your broker would have to do a margin call, meaning to tell you to think about where your money went to, as this is a risk to your livelihood and the need for more money or a different strategy.

After we know the risks or perils, we can look at what moves the ES-futures market, or will and could make it move, then hopefully, one can sperate, in that hopefully money can come from the ES market continually.

We could place a trade when the market moves and make money moving with the market. So we need to know the market and what would move the market to forecast which way the market will go.

I think, from experience, that the ES-futures market is moved by major economic events. Economic news that moves one market in the commodities futures markets may not effect all commodities the same. Oil futures may move differently than silver futures, that is why I watch mostly ES-futures closely to get the feel for one commodity's market dispositions. The different economic events are listed on an Economic Calendar, that is basically world wide and fuel changes in the markets based on fundamental analysis.

A search on the internet bewrays that, everyone can see the Economic Calendar. When the Federal Reserves cuts the interest rate by one-half of a percentage point then that event will be moving the markets. A Federal Reserve meeting will be on the Economic Calendar, so traders will be waiting for it, to see what happens.

News events can also move the markets as what happened on the evening of June 12, 2025 when Israel attacked Iran and Iran responded. This happened in pre-market trading hours and ES-futures went down about 100 points, 50 points at about thirty minutes after the ES-futures open. The chart looked like it could go down and it in fact did go down. Those trades that had the ability to short the market made money and the time to do this was important, just as how long the reaction would take effect or to find the bottom here in this example.

There can be a market: scudding, with a slow reaction or both, depending on what's happening in different time frames. The time frame you trade in (when you buy and sell) is important because you will need different risk capital to allow you to trade in each different one. One needs to not make ES trading personal, if the emotion is in oneself and it comes out, then it is hard to keep your rules and trade consistently.

Just day trading ES-futures can allow or require less capital in your account. This is different than keeping the same position from a day trade to extending it as an overnight trade, then you'll need more risk capital. This is a rule, because overnight trading is more risky. One will want to keep their capital safe, so this is a rule one would need to understand. One should only trade when they are allowed to do so with the amount of money in their account. Because trading ES-futures, I believe, is a privilege and not to be taken lightly. Another rule that I think is important for me is to, only trade once in a session. Next, make more rules like, make a rule as to how long to wait before you go into a trade.

Taking time to see the pattern is so really important. As you need a conscious pattern to trade and that is in your time frame so you can leave a trade in the market. If everyone knows, or feels, that the market is going up, watch out, because the market might have to cycle down before it goes to where you want it, to go up. When this happens your intuition will let you know. Some traders may want to paper trade to get the feel of the market and the time frame they want to trade in. This is just codifying your intuition with knowledge.

Your intuition is another rule you should have for trading ES-futures. If you get intuition that the market is going up, then you might want to doubt yourself to say the opposite. I have done a recording of SV analysis in about three minutes and get an indication when I listen to my +reverse speech+ or SV to do one trade, but the market goes the other way. At this time, currently, my account is not closed, as there is still just below $1000 in it, just sitting there until I can refund it to $5000. The market went the other way, as I trained myself to doubt my intuition probably by the way I did my SV. This book is, therefore, to fix this and not doubt my intuition, but SV will still be helpful for other things as long as SV doesn't cross-up the information.

I have found from reviewing my SV that my intuition can get crossed-up to the opposite, a +parallax.+ My intuition, I can hear in SV, is encoded in my CV and can be captured by recording my CV, out my mouth. I then can be recording my CV and reversing it in my audio editor, with the reverse effect, to get my SV. This is where I SV my intuition, as this is the topic of my conservation in CV, to try to see where the ES-futures will go. My higher self can tell me the direction of the market in SV and also with the feeling or sixth sense of where it is going to go. If I do both, intuition and SV, then it can flip or +parallax+ to the opposite, so I should never SV my intuition before a trade! My intuition and my +Meself+ in SV must be two different things. My intuition can get crossed and spit out the opposite if SV is done to it. Next time I can trade, I will have a rule of not doing SV before my trade, as it can go and +parallax+ to the other way from foreknowledge. So, I will use this prescious of my intuition by itself.

[In the next quote I have highlighted the problem of trading and not knowing why I'm loosing money. Is my subconscious trading or am I?]

> Listening to SV from the searching of intuition in CV will lead to the opposite in SV. Because the CV intuition is transformed by a reflection back into SV to give the opposite. I think this is the reason why I'm losing so much money trading ES-futures. I would trade ES-Futures using SV to do what my **+Meself+** says, I would focus on the short term and miss the long term trend because I would be trading against the long term market movement. **~It seemed logical but there are ogres.~ ~Matt when you try to talk and see which way ES will go get the opposite. Hurry back and jettison and you can win Matthew. Matt when you put your intuition in you get the opposite.~** So I should trade when I get the insight and place the trade, then do SV afterwards! [*, p.202]

The Flow of Information Through a Zero Point

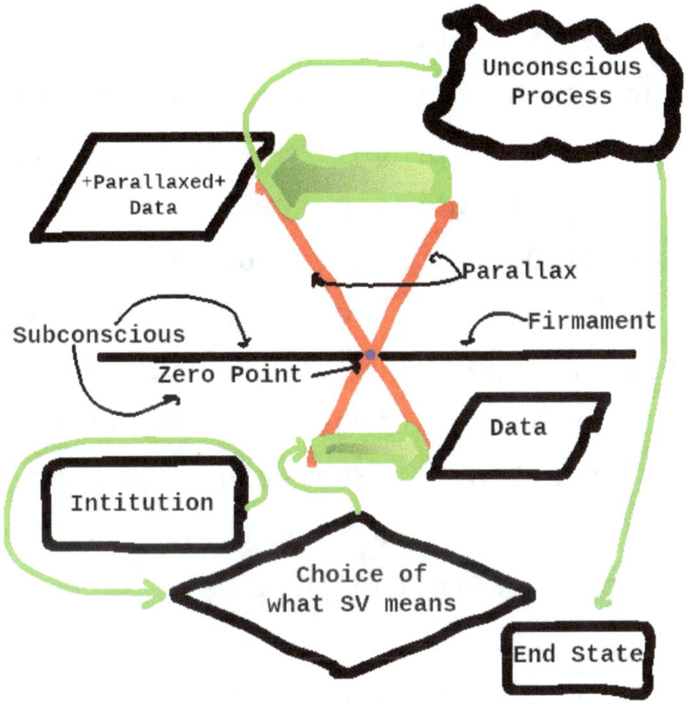

Flowchart 1: How SV can flip the intuition to get the opposite when trading ES-futures is because of the +parallax+ between this earthly world and the spiritual world.

Flowchart 1, shows how the seemingly straight forward process of SV is more complicated then I first thought. If I think with my CV about my intuition (as in important data of where the market is going), do SV on that, and then my intuition is getting transformed in the unconscious to give the opposite. Because the intuition is spiritual and the market point value is physical. This combining things together like this is a tool of +Say-tin,+ in that one can be tricked with the blending of the spirit with the physical.

There is a lost sheep situation like daydreaming and thinking vanity. The physical CV thought is in the R3DT, indicated by the small green arrow to the right and the spiritual is the large green arrow to the left. There was a change of wanting something, from going from the R3DT to the 5D, like taking candy from a baby, that is what +Say-tin+ does. I guess that the 5D is a bigger space than the R3DT and getting there is like going through a pin hole or zero point. Perception with intuition and being in the present is important for communication, as shown in the story from my own experience with a “dog-ie” I knew.

This dog was my landlord's dog and I called him, “little dog-ie” and now I think he did not think of himself as little. I had a dream of him and he was big, to show me his real size, and hint hint, it was not little. The dream, I believe, is in the 5D with our astral bodies. So when I went there in the 5D I got the message that he did not think of himself as small and I can respect that, but things in the 5D were bigger. In order to go to the 5D we must, I think, go through the zero point as the zero point is a hole to a new set of dimensions at a higher frequency then our realm, the R3DT. We have size and a top and bottom. Well, I think that to go through the zero point the top and bottom and everywhere in between reflect into the 5D, by going through the zero point, so we would be upside down, along lines of +parallax.+

The +parallax+ occurs in the brain and the universe, as we are all connected we have this image as an archetype to creation. The black line divides the two realms and only the zero point can let anything through, between the 5D and R3DT, our thoughts can travel through the zero point. +Say-tin+'s bad intuition is knowledge, this is what Adam and Eve got.

+Say-tin+'s intuition was from below and Adam and Eve's intuition was only from above. When +Say-tin+'s intuition combined with Adam and Eve's intuition a +parallax+ occurred, because both were in conscious focus and as a result, Adam and Eve then got the opposite answer. Instead of life they got death, when they bit into that apple, an apple of +parallax.+

Wisdom is as to intuition and the spiritual as death is to physical or the R3DT and if focused intuition is processed in the brain with SV then the SV will find the opposite to be true.

The solution is then to take your time and get distracted into something else, record your CV to get both spiritual and physical, then do SV to find the truthful advice that pops into your conscious. Don't let your right side (wisdom) know what the left side (death) is doing, adapted from the "Gospel of Thomas."

The ES-futures market might be listening to itself and wander and find the right way. There are cycles to the market, but afterwards the signposts show-up. There are Fibonacci point levels that show the grander patterns. So if the market consciously knew those Fibonacci point levels there would be no need for the market. Likewise, I should not be thinking consciously of the market and where it is going to go,

I should just live my life doing something else and then when I do SV on that, the message will come in and I can act on it.

The market might have to position itself to go for the daily trend. So if I don't wait and ponder when to enter the market, then I will have to take the loss at the mercy of the market, (I'm too early) until the trend goes in my favor. The daily trend, my Dad said, can appear after the first 15 minutes from the opening bell. That is to say, scilicet, why I need to take my time and just trade once per trading day.

I have my higher self trying to help me because it was a shock the last time I lost my money. Each time I lose money, then it gets worse and increasing horribleness the next time. I just need to take my time. Sometimes I wonder if my brain is damaged. If my brain is damaged then I can custom make my rules to benefit me in the best possible ways. So if my rules work, then don't fix them.

If this mental ability is damaged or undeveloped then one might have personality disorders, for example, the narcissist or the introvert. The **+meself+** is really our smarter unconscious half and doesn't want to interfere in the **+ogres+** so that they can play and learn in one's life environment. If the **+meself+** was dominant then this person might be a savant or indigo child, otherwise I suppose if we do stupid things, then the **+meself+** will want to die or leave because it has no way to cause any conscious messages other than intuition. I think one goal of SBTM/SV is to help reveal the **+meself,+** since this might help

> people who have no access to it in their lives or too much. [*, p.127]

I don’t want my +Meself+ to die. If I don’t have my higher self, that is like loosing my Soul and I would fall in the cracks of society, not to be seen or heard by normal people again. Perhaps my +Meself+ is just my future self coming towards me.

When an event happens, the circumstances to the event might have to congeal in the future before the event gets to the present. So the past is connected to the future and the present is just a loop bringing everything together. To be able to witness this in the conscious present time we need to take our time, to get this intuition.

And Be Capital Safe by Making Money

So, before I trade next time, one rule will be to take my time. I thought I could make my money back, but that was really hard since the state of my mind changed into a non-trading mind. I was in a state of mini-craziness and time did cure this wound. So how am I coming back, this choice of rules has everything to do with it. I want to succeed and make what I deserve and I want to respect the ES-futures market. In the past failures, I was trading against myself as based on a lie, believing my Ego or any bad spirit that had penetrated into my mind or +whirlwind,+ hence going against, Matt, or my conscious self. So besides that, the other traders in the market are numerous, as the ES-futures market is huge.

In the above underline I found in SV: **~Should we say? That the ES is run by Say-tin, sad.~** This means that the top trader in ES is +Say-tin+ and I cannot over or under estimate this, and I believe it to be true. I should keep this on my mind, and not trade just by myself, but require my +Meself+ to help me trade. Because I will not be able to trade better than +Say-tin,+ while I think my +Meself+ can averruncate it, to ward it, off with my rules. I will trade just once per trading session, as I will remember this. Now back to my book.

Some traders are automated A.I. computer algorithms that make trades for big institutions, as in hedge funds and governments. A.I. is a lot bigger than people think. Billionaires are not going to tell the normal people what they are doing. They can probably turn on a water faucet with A.I.'s help trading ES-futures and gush out money. [As the next quote shows, these billionaires are capable of having resources and connections to make certain things happen in the world that may not be seen by the general public.]

~. . .do I think that A.I. will take over the world, that is a negative. . .trying to get enough qubits to crack encryption, error correction is killing it. . .On the contrary, there is an A.I. to crack encryption and it is at ********.~**

~Right now A.I. at this stage can't learn, it will require a lot more money. . .there could be world war to figure out who owns A.I., probably. . . whoever owns A.I. will be invincible. . .~

~. . .the problem with reverse speech is that there is not a lot of details, please. . .~ ~Whoever controls A.I., it is going to be a game. . .whoever controls A.I. will control the world, very certainty. . .~ ~Whoever controls A.I., it will be a seg-ga, a lot of money. . .~

~. . .some aliens are helping us create A.I. to get us on the right track, we just need to give them a lot of money. . .~

~Sometimes I don't know what I'm saying about A.I., sorry for that man.~

~On this I'm certain about A.I., one day we are dead man. . .Matt Mandell if you reverse speech me I have an issue.~ [*, pp.143-144]

There are some companies that want to hedge with the ES-futures, as well as including some mutual funds for retirement saving accounts. Further down the chain I think there are traders on the floor, in Chicago, at the exchange that trades ES-futures. As there must be CME floor traders that take the other side or it might be all electronic, as this is outside the scope for this book. At the lowest level there is me, with just trading one lot per trading session, speculating not hedging.

I started, thinking about trading ES-futures in 2018 and received my first 1099-B for the 2019 tax year from trading ES-futures. I have lost money each year and then refunded my account the next year, after a break in trading from failure. Because I always felt that I was not trading when I was loosing money, something came over me and I did not want to quit, because afterwards I thought, *That was not me.* I wanted to break out of it. This time will be different, as I will trade for me and I'm trying to show this for you in this book. Next time, I will not look back and proclaim that, *That was me trading.*

About 2018, I tried futures trading with S&P 500 "ES" lots. I found myself trading the opposite to the market. When I thought to just go the other way, part of myself would not relent and I would incredibly still trade the wrong way. At one time I did trade the right way, but incredibly I somehow deep down did not feel I was worthy to make so much money.

Another failure happened. However, for those interested, I looked into using the Fibonacci levels, as those who can are probably the ones who make money. I was also looking at the oscillators and selling at the top and buying at the bottoms, when they would overshoot. I would recommend starting by funding your account with at least $5,000 to $20,000 dollars of cash and then make one trade a day.

Hopefully, trade in the morning and get out at the end of the day or the same times each day. Because once your in, you can ride it all day long if the market is going one direction. I'm writing this book to convey the basic information to others of SBTM/SV that I have found, trading 'ES' futures is one way to do this. Information can come to you from an internal voice.

ES-Futures trading rules for me: (1) Only trade once you see the pattern. This might take the whole first hour to observe the market trading, (2) Do use hints from your own intuition and also from the **+meself,+** (3) Use the Order Cancels Order feature, (4) Don't trade on a holiday and (5) Be capital safe.

This internal voice can include the **+meself,+** ego and **+ogres+** and so these may not serve me very well on their own. It is better to combine one's "ego" into the **+meself+** so that they become one. [*, p. 89]

Today is Sunday September 22, 2024 and I proclaim to myself and my +Meself+ that I will not fall into this trap, trading against my rules, again. [I did fail, by losing money on some big trades that I thought was right, I should have been strong enough to get out with a stop and take the loss]. What is so important is to know that, I will take my time. Follow the rules to make my life easier I think is true. If I know the rules then life gets easier.

My current Rules are: (1) take your time so I can see it, let the market come to me so I'm on time, just need one level of the market depth to watch, live; (2) only trade once per day, Monday thru Friday; (3) make a trade when I get the signal and then get out of the trade after I check my SV (because SV can be asynchronism of the small movements I want to see in the market); (4) I need to be capital safe, cut a check for the reason "account maintenance" when my account gets to over $14,000; and lastly (5) make a log here or next book to document what feeling is right and true. I don't want to rely on my memory of past behaviors and the trading outcomes, because I need to record it here to start my success. If I can be advertent to the moves of the market, be heedful to the signal, then I can get a feeling for said market.

To find the rules the trader needs to know how many times they will trade a day and for what time interval. This is just to find a pattern in the market and look for that pattern. If the trader has rules for one pattern but decides today to be impatient and trade in a different patten, they might fail. One pattern I looked at, because I noticed it, was the volume for the day as the futures traded. Sometimes when the volume, at a level, got to and went over 666 or 667 then it would increase. If this volume went to 666 and then traded at lower levels then it would go lower.

Another pattern is using your first impression, intuition, after your login to your trading system, or before. Ask the question, "Is the chart looking to go up or down?" If this is your rule then this might work a profit for you. This could be an example of scalping in a short term, as in a few minutes, and then don't trade anymore the whole day. These are some simple rules, but the **+morphine+** might convince you to make new rules, then you loose your profit.

Another way is to do SV, but to use the conscious to access the intuition one has and read the market's general direction. That is why having a margin to be able to hold a trade over to the next day is important. Being able to keep a trade to the next day will release stress and this can allow for sober thought to know the direction. Planning on one trade a day for a few hours, and do something else, is the safest way to trade if the trader has rules to do this. The intuition knows where the market will go, making small trades with one lot of "ES," then look at the market again when you are done with the something you were doing, and see the end trade. This might be the best way to make money in futures for someone who can't conceive of it.

Trading after the night's open at 5 p.m. ~~Eastern~~ [Central] time, offers low volume and a better chance of it moving and not jumping to new levels. This is from my experience in the month of November, 2023. **~God forbid you to make more than one trade a day Mathyou.~** I'm not sure who told me this, but usually my **+Meself+** will have my name in the SV to let me know it is him. On July, 10, 2024, I heard a SV

> indicating that I would be fooling myself that God told me to do something. [*, pp. 152-153]

I thought that, *This cannot be so, did God communicate with me?* Yes. +Say-tin+ must of came into my +whirlwind+ to try to convince me that God would not think me important or God doesn't talk to too many things. Only +Say-tin+ would mean to make God far from me. I want to know God and not +Say-tin+ and evil things with images from him. I just have to wrestle with my faith and make this a fact, to myself, just trade ES one time a day and conceive of making money for this one trade.

Table 2:

List of common +S-M+s and story-lines

+Alfred+: This is referring to a middle aged man.

+*basura*+: It means you are stinking. Note: I looked up *basura* and translated, it means “garbage” in Spanish.

+caldera+: A hole that once crossed will be going into it. Because once made and lost, that will need to be remade again. **~Foresight helps you get out of the caldera.~**

+canopy+: The covering above the subconscious, evidently the subconscious is just below the **+canopy.+**

+cast-a-lan+: A bad way to go, you’re casting-a-life away!

+cen-ta-meter+: This is referring to a one-in-a-hundred chance.

+chev-ie+: The male's reproductive organ. **~Matt that is where the soul is at, same for the +Tab-a-tha+ Matt.~** Having the soul in this area during reproduction or sex allows the parent's souls to attract the soul of the child during sex.

+cinnamin+: This is a sin that is small, a baby sin.

+cyclops+: If someone tries to talk trash and they are not good at it because it comes out bad. This person is not taking to the audience, if they continue they are eventually going to become insane. For example, "I'm not going to live the dream, I sleep with it. When someone asks, "How I'm doing, I tell them I live my life like I mean it!" as Matt Mandell showed his teeth. Alternatively, since the cyclops has only one eye, it can't see the other side to a situation and might make the wrong choice.

+dare-re queen+: There is an event that is cooking. It is at first hot and then going, as the host is a woman, but the party turns cold. Some guests may be like, "What happened, I did not expect that?" Some may like the cool-off, but others may be surprised and leave the party.

+de-mon+: From my experience this is an Earth spirit. The **+de-mon+** wants tragedy just look in their ghostly face and you can tell from their expression they are deviant and will do harm.

+ding+: The stock price goes up.

+don't reverse speech me+: Some people have trouble when their BTM is done onto them. This is evidence that we are all connected. I think most people are frightened of this **+ocean.+** With BTM the right to privacy is important because it might be a timeless encounter, especially if the chakras are open. If someone is connected with thoughts of another then, "When is this disconnected?" Someone may feel that they know the person who BTM them, because this story-line has been found many times before. Therefore, it is the ethical decision to remember who these people are, on a list, and don't record them again in the future, if asked to. So when recording someone in person ask for their permission and explain BTM, if you do that.

+Easter bunny+: **~Means that you are always losing money, it just goes down the hole man.~**

+Evil wind+: Someone or something is conducting a psychic attack on you. A symptom is an unexplained tiredness or headache.

+gossamer+: It functions to shield from open chakras, which I believe are above the head, shaped in a corkscrew form. The **+gossamer+** from the **+selfs,+** is a sort of sunscreen film all over the body. This sunscreen will get worn down weekly while listening to SBTM/SV and that is why the **+sacrament+** is important to uphold, by resting at least one day a week. Because keeping the **+sacrament+** will allow for repair of the **+gossamer.+**

+helter-skelter+: Things will get crazy.

+hen-a-see+: You are drunk and probably will make a bad decision.

+I+: This could be the ego part of the subconscious. On November 1, 2023 I edited all my +S-M+ of the **+me+** into an **+I.+** Then, I changed it, for the **+me+** to ego on June 30, 2025! I still believe that the **+meself+** +S-M+ is specifically associated with the higher-self.

+knee-deep+: Is the notice that you are in the **+whirlwind,+** as it is liquid, and up to your knees in it, the subconscious **+ocean,+** as they say.

+liquid-de+: Is the communing of two or more spirits, as the waters can combine or two frequencies combine to make a new frequency. **+Liquid-de+** can't happen unless consent is given (somewhere) because the two frequencies are added together not subtracted, this is because of the concept of free will.

+lost in the sauce+: I imagine some cocktail sauce and there is a piece of shrimp in it that I'm trying to find. I lost my direction, and just randomly or even gambling, try and find the piece's location. I need to solve my problem.

+It's Ali Baba+: There will be a loss of profit due to the antagonist present in this novel. They may win this time.

+man-be-pam-be+: This man is a slippery decision maker because he has trouble making the decision, to execute, and actually make something happen when the time comes.

~Matt Mandell if I get into your whirlwind you are screwed~: When I heard this during a BTM, I stopped. Because this is the ethical reason not to BTM someone if they give an unconditioned stop. They can add information to your BTM in your day-to-day life and those around you will unconsciously pick it up. If the one in your **+whirlwind+** wants to do you harm then even if you are the nicest good person around others, you can still get the bad end of the stick!

+me+: On February 3, 2024 I'm not really sure. As of June 30, 2024, I think the **+me+** is the ego, as in **^. . .the me is trying to help you. . .^**

+meself+: This is the higher spirit that is in the crown chakra. I found on June 13, 2023 in SV that my **+Meself+** was female, **~Yea, your +Meself+ is female, Matt.~** This male-female duality is familiar from reading ancient texts. In my opinion, a female in the flesh will probably have a male spirit **+meself, +** and vice versa for a male in the flesh.

+mill-a-meter+: This is a one-in-a-thousand chance.

+Mir-re+: The communication of the subconscious. **+Mir-re+** can bring peace to the Earth because we all, or will be able to, speak the same thought-language.

+moon-shine+: Possibility, or maybe, a light at the end of the tunnel.

+morphine+: That drug that makes us feel good, but as a consequence it will make us follow through with bad decisions. **~Morphine metaphor lets you know something is wrong, Matthew.~**

+net-scape+: There is a landscape that will go up then down resembling a city with buildings or rolling hills in the distance. **~. . .it is going sideways Matthew.~**

+nic-a-load-de-in+: I'm loading a program or new life/career that will be good and in the process, **-load** or loading is the before the first day of work and **-in** is the part where the new career takes off inside of me. The **-de** means it is all over me. Since this metaphor may refer to a cartoon channel this career should be fun to watch. It could also mean I'm a kid.

+nickel backer+: A cat's anus. "Look at this cat." The person referenced to this is nice and even likable in the face, however the situation can or will want to turn and show the nickel at the back end.

+ogre+: **~Ogres around you can put images in your mind, Matthew.~** **+Ogre+** reportedly can destroy man and might be connected to man, to serve as a lower-self. **~By centering the mind you can get rid of the ogre.~ ~When you think the**

wrong thoughts you get the ogres.~ ~When the ogres come in they are always wrong.~

+quick-sand+: Shut the mouth, you can't say anything to pull you out!

+pair-rot+: Listening or watching media and not letting logic correct the playback in one's life, this person can't help themselves correct, it is the vanity of vanity. **+red venom+**: **~Red venom means there will be blood, Matthey.~**

+Reverse speech is magnetic.+: Meaning that the closer one is to another, as a magnetic pole attracts stronger the closer it is to the opposite pole then, they can communicate through the **+whirlwind.+** To help concentrate just say to yourself without talking, **+Reverse speech is magnetic.+** and this helps focus and center communication with your thoughts telepathically, in the 5D to someone or thing.

+Reverse speech is not specific, full stop.+: Meaning, making the information heard with SBTM/SV into printed words of advice sometimes fails when time is necessary to form a conclusion. Sometimes when SBTM/SV predicts an outcome it is opposite or does not happen when you think it will happen. The possibility is that SBTM/SV sees this possibility however there are other events that may need to happen first, usually. The fewer additional interactions required allows the prediction to be more accurate. Because, **~Reverse speech is all-encompassing.~**

+Reverse speech me.+: Some people have trouble when their BTM is done onto them. Maybe not this time, but because you might of already asked for their permission and explained BTM to them.

+The problem with reverse speech is that it is not specific.+: Meaning that this is a repeated SBTM/SV, from above, which usually happens when doing SBTM/SV. This means one does not need to listen to a whole hour of SBTM/SV because there are repeated parts, much the way a dream repeats to get the information into consciousness. Sometimes the repeated SBTM/SV will add information from before, as this results into a story-line. With the theory of the story-line, as it builds onto thoughts, we have the opportunity to decipher +S-M+s because of the added information and we should also become aware of the dark side, in that someone who knows their unconscious well can be giving us false information in the story-line, to trick others unconsciously.

+sacrament+: This is not listening to SBTM/SV on Sunday.

+scarecrow+: Someone without a mind to think on their own. This can be accomplished by taking fentanyl, the death of the brain.

+See you in the whirlwind.+: The **+whirlwind+** is that two dimensional transition between this 3D reality to other higher dimensions that make up the universe. I believe we live in a bilevel universe, one level is the ordinary reality of our 3D and the other is the unseen reality of 5D, 7D, complex numbers and quantum dynamics. So knowing about this transition means that I can mediate some information that can transition between these two levels of existence. **+Whirlwind+** is the gateway to the other dimensions of our Universe. The universe vibrates to a singularity and back again to the R3DT. I found this by thinking through the different scenarios with OSA. OSA starts with something objective, say E=Mvv or Einstein's Mass-Energy equivalency formula, then examines what if this is the basis for something not yet analyzed to explain other phenomena. My OSA shows that a transform in dimensions allows for transforming time into a frequency. The end result of this OSA is that, without time there are dimensions that have frequency instead. We are all one without time and can sync-up and exchange information as another new frequency, since frequency changes here and not time. As a result, the **+whirlwind+** accessed with SBTM/SV can connect to all people. Practical use: If you hear your thought in the **+whirlwind,+** doing SV, then just repeat it to yourself and it will eventually come true.

+sand-bagged+: Getting **+sand-bagged+** means an accident is about to happen. You got evil spirits trying to put psychic +war-fair+ on you.

+sandman+: They might work for the government.

+seg-ga+: A new life to play the game.

+self+: This is equivalent to the **+I+** as the subconscious voice in one's head, I think it sits somewhere in the brain.

+server+: This probably is, by definition, someone who gives, by a connection of at least two things together. **~Yea Matt each person has a server in their head.~ ~The server works as you need it. . .~** The **+server+** doesn't serve you it helps you access the unconsciousness. **~The server is located in the cerebellum, Matt.~** So, the server could "serve" your thoughts to you.

+skelle-wag+: Probably a lost sailor or sailor who is shipwrecked.

+shapeshifter+: This is possibly a spirit around someone, as taking control of their aura, and they can try to control other minds by being the leader of others. **~One way to tell a +shapeshifter+ is that they don't like to look into your eye Mathe.~**

+shinding+: This is when a stock goes down then up, usually at the opening bell. For instance, a stock gets shorted overnight for the open and then, perhaps, the brokerages are party to the other side and make the stock price go back up.

+sheep-server+: **~Matt you are a sheep-server because you don't know who is talking to ya.~** **~Matt you are a sheep-server because you don't listen.~** My SV for me is hard to know when a hostile force is communicating to me. Then I make the wrong choice, because I'm quick to make a choice, sometimes I don't listen. **~Please take your time, it's in the +whirlwind+ for ya.~ ~Sheep-server is from your ego, boss.~ ~Sheep-server is always wrong man.~ ~My definition of sheep-**

server is that it will always lead you astray.~

+shel-he-rack+: **~Means that you hurt your back, Math-tha.~**

+shotgun+ and **+shot-group+**: A 5D shot that is not specific in detail, it is when you hit around the target in R3DT. Having better intuition will give a better and smaller **+shot-group+** with your **+shotgun+** by picking the right way, not opposite. **~The third eye is the +Shotgun+ Maththe.~**

+simba+: I'm committing a sin, but, there is a good reason for doing so.

+simp-son+: To think or make a prediction on surface terms, not delving into or discerning anything else than what you first conjecture. Taking advice from fear or speed in answering a question. This sounds like it's the same as **+sheep-server.+**

+snakehead+: I think, this is following the orders from Satin in one's mind. To move people from

point A to point B, probably not the best advice, use your own intuition.
+snakewoman+: Not a real woman, unusually smart, and a serpent.

+source+: **~Source will help who you are today, full-stop.~ ~If you don't have a source then you tend to go insane.~ ~Source is namesake. . .a source over you, full-stop.~ ~Source gets you faith, this stop the wolf.~ ~Source is who you try to contact Matthey, don't source anyone other than Jesus.~ ~For ya Jesus Christ is source . . . his message is easy.~ ~Some people's source is Satin. He will sue you Matthew.~ ~Whatever is in your source gives your spirit power.~ ~Source connects you to your whirlwind, just to let you know.~**

+surf-side+: Means that things are going to start moving.

+tab-a-tha+: The woman's reproductive organ.

+T-Rex+: As in Tyrannosaurus or "tyranny," is leadership or a leader. Probably some evil in the World Government. I found in SV that the **+T-Rex+** or the World Leader lives in an underground city in Earth. **~You are right, there is an underground city and they don't want you to let that out.~**

+Tri-say-ra-tops!+: Is Satin or the Devil and is very ferocious but easily runs away when confronted, or revealed, for what it is. Satin has two horns, but the person saying this with their tongue is the third horn. It is Satin talking to you!

+urlslia+: For me, possibly a trans-human or **+snakewoman.+** If you hear this, then I recommend to stay away from her. **~Urlslia, a woman with a flat chest. . .~** Evidently, I also heard that it is something different in these women's genetic code. Also from my experience, talking to a **+urlslia,+** it can be tough because there could be a **+caldera+** waiting for me, try to walk away. **~Matt when she heard you come in with your music, it was the wrong music.~** Else, for me, I found she had to get away from me, so pay attention to who has to leave from you when you enter a place. I think an **+urlslia+** could be a feminist.

+wolf+: **~Wolf is what devours you Matt.~** **~A wolf is like an ogre, but different.~**

+whirlwind+: Your **+Meself+** can communicate with you through your **+whirlwind,+** that energy from the connection to higher dimensions and can spread over the all. **~The whirlwind translates it. . .messages from the other side.~** **~Matthew, it is very important to know that the thoughts you put into your head, the whirlwind serves it.~** **~Matthew, the whirlwind is a gestalt, its the parts that come together, Matthew.~** **~The whirlwind is just a reflection of your self Matt.~** If Satin gets into your **+whirlwind+** then, because the **+whirlwind+** is not of the R3DT, when you speak your conscious, then you could unknowingly use this reflection of Satin in your **+whirlwind+** and think it is you! **~Be afraid of Lucifer, because if he gets into your whirlwind he can talk for ya.~** **~If Lucifer is in your whirlwind then say, Help Jesus, Lucifer get out.~** [*, pp. 130-138]

Chapter 0: About the Subresonate Voice, (SV)

The SV is one's subconscious voice, recorded then played back in reverse direction to hear the subconscious, is an important function to live a life, for some people. I guess I'm a +simp-son+ and have no life. For instance, SV helps me know about my behavior and SV can act as a guide to live a better life. I use SV to uncover my grief and realize I have had a lot of defeats in life and quit, I get in SV that I'm a +simp-son.+ So I have proofread my manuscript for this book in my own voice to edit it and also find out about myself. I have also thought it incumbent on me to promote a writing style for documenting SV. [Below I have a writing style to depict SV and I will include the same style in this book, as I'm continuing my writing style from my first book.]

> The purpose to know your own psyche is because it can give you important information. This information I recommend to be stylistically represented, with subconscious metaphors in +pluses+, story-lines in ~tildes,~ Subconscious Channeling (SC) in ^carets^ and telepathy in *asterisks.* For SV, I recommend a standard to describe what the Subconscious Metaphors (+S-M+) are by enclosing them in pluses and then SV phrases as story-lines enclosed in tildes. However, it depends on the one doing the SBTM or SV, their state of mind and their ability to decipher the subconscious to find this information.
>
> I define normal speaking as the Conscious Voice (CV). CV is from the spoken voice transmitted by air to the ears. We use CV when we are objective, non-telepathic and in a state of consciously hearing and interacting with others. [*, p.11]

Sometimes listening to your own CV helps you stop for a moment and try to think more clearly. This is intuition coming out of you and you just need to try and listen then reflect by stopping and rethinking it or say it out loud. Sometimes we want to discount the intuition and do the opposite, like not listening. The chakras should be understood to know your intuition, as they are energy. Disconnected chakras can have trouble fending off psychic attacks by not being in tune with yourself. For example if I had a psychic attack, I might then get a bad back because my chakras were misaligned by the psychic attack.

Then ask yourself, *Why the bad back now?,* and the answer could be because there was a psychic energy around you and you needed to get a message from the subconscious to change your ways. The psychic energy needs to be grounded out, that is a gud reason to be calm.

12-3-3 I recently had this information received by me that there is an organization run by humans, and they rule the money system. I have found that they might be the ones conducting a psychic warfare on me, so that I do not make money on my investments. The reason why this is, might be, is because they can distort my thinking.

Distorted thinking can come about by damaging my chakras and this can allow for bad intuition. Well, I'm starting to see through this, from trial and error. The best way to fight it is to eat right, keep a daily routine, don't break the sabbath and know the consequences of one's thoughts so that they are not dragged down into the lower energies of the R3DT frequencies. [*, pp. 111-112]

Intuition might be bad and cause you to double check your gud intuition and then switch to your bad intuition. There can be psychic attacks going on, something I don't necessarily understand. If someone can get into your +whirlwind+ then they can program you, in the subconscious, and you might not be consciously becoming aware of it. An indicator of a psychic attack is someone looking into your pupils, then they do something. Whatever they do, they will be having you on their mind because they just looked at you. Another indicator of a psychic attack is a headache or grumpiness. These are actions at a distance and they are conducted through the +whirlwind.+

Sometimes you are psychically attacked and you do not see the person, however you could be seeing an image or feeling in your brain from the pineal gland or third eye. You could be having a headache. Once again, someone is having you on their mind and you should be aware. Find the source of this probe. To do this you have to know what you or their original innate feelings were. For instance your soul is innate to you, so a frustrating thought could be innate to your +whirlwind+ or theirs.

> 28-3 **~. . .I see that the ribosomes looks like it helps the souls communicate, Matthe.~. . .~Your soul in this life has a purposes, Matthe.~. . .~To your body your soul is innate.~ ~Good for the soul is parsnips.~** [*, p.164]

Listening to your own +reverse speech+ is terrific, it might do things we don't know to the body. One can do SV and find information from their higher self, mystical information. My +Meself,+ in a anagogic way can communicate to me in the SV, from above, was trying to tell me to eat more vegetables as the leafy produce from the garden can help my body center to itself because it's working better. Memories can be decoded with SV when the body is able to have information flow through it.

SV can find memories and you can remember past greatness and also personal shame. SV can invoke automnesia of what one did and even find some information on past lives. What is covered can be uncovered with

SV. Besides remembering yourself you can remember the market and what it did to you.

Trading ES-futures can have an impact on one's health, as it can be stressful if the trade goes the wrong way and the trader is loosing money. There is a threshold that determines how much money was lost, as in: a one time trade that looses a lot or a set of smaller trades that loose a little each time. The blood pressure can rise, in my experience, and then I could not think correctly to trade. Being calm is one reason to take your time, because you want to see the trade. My +Meself+ said, **~Take you time and let the market come to you.~** One should not rely on someone else to give themselves intuition on a trade.

One should have a natural conscious intuition and take time to know it verses relying onto other's subconscious and being quick with decisions.

Listening to other's +reverse speech+ is bad and there might be fear to make a quick choice from it. I call listening and taking apart someone's +reverse speech,+ as Back Track Mechanics (BTM) and can understand that you would be becoming +liquid-de+ with their psychic energies. You would have to clear the offending spirit or energies out, primary by changing your behavior and secondarily by just doing SV. [By doing SV, as described on the quote below, I found these subconscious SV quotes important to realize about the power of being calm.]

If we were in a higher dimensional set then we could imagine a 3D object moving around the loop. Assuming one would need to add one dimension to get a dimension then one would need to add at least three to our R3DT to get to the higher plane in the universe, or 5D. Since in the R3DT, I can imagine a point on two dimensions adding three to this would total five. That is my proof that the higher set of dimensions is a 5D set. So if we add the real three dimensions to 5 . . .

I found doing SV on the above underline is: **~Yah that's right I conduit through your whirlwind that's how I hear you, boss. Ya speak up because this is stuff is very hot hot-hot it is a proof of concept. Now follow through. Follow through, Matthew.~**

Note: I need to be calm and this will open the **+whirlwind+** so I can hear my **+Meself+** clearly without distractions of unfamiliar spirits, when I'm doing SV. Continuing from the paragraph:

[. . .]D that is eight dimensions and we need three more to get to the eleven of String Theory. I think that these additional three dimensions, outside the real 3D and 5D, are used to contain[. . .]

I found doing SV on the above underline is: **~Serenity. With serenity we can move through ya, Me profit!~**

Note: This seems to indicate that if I don't do BTM on other people then I don't have those people's **+whirlwind'+**s causing psychic warfare on me! I have not done BTM on another person for about three days and I notice a difference of being less on an edge. I don't have to worry about someone's spirit attacking me and now this allows the **+whirlwind+** to have a better connection for my own higher-self to come through more clearly. Continuing on with the paragraph:

[. . .]the real three dimensions and 5D together.[. . .]

I found doing SV on the above underline was: **~Hey. He happened to**

send this information from the whirlwind. Ask and you shall receive.~ [*, pp. 33-34]

Doing SV is new for humans and proof-of-concept, if I or someone else can start making money trading ES with it. If I start to make money then the paradigm of working two dead end jobs could be over if other people can listen to SV too. They will be gathering subconscious information. From hunter-gather to the industrial revolution and then onto the subconscious-gathering with an A.I. revolution, on this Earth. The disguised alien ETs would have their power structure skewed and a new reality for many folks, from doing the daily grind in our visible dimensions. We live in a reality of 26 dimensions and the subconscious is partly in the future, that is why the subconscious is faster than the conscious. I have a Grand Unified Theory (GUT) of the universe to help understand where are the spiritual and physical, to help show that SV can have relevant information for oneself.

It is easy to assume that the other dimensions of String Theory are curled up and out of sight from the R3DT. Since the detection of the other imaginary dimensions have not been found, maybe, eight dimensions have not been forth coming (10D - 2ID), then I will assume that they are not curled up, but are larger or at a higher energy than the R3DT, as in curled out. However, I really think the 10D are smaller because I believe that there is a set of five dimensions at a higher energy, or slower time, than the R3DT and that these are connected to the R3DT with a worm hole. This is how we get to this coupled five dimensional set or 5D. 5D, consequently, is at a higher energy because it is timeless and also probably in the future

> compared to the R3DT. There is a GUT to explain this logically. This GUT can be used to show communication between zero points.
>
> I'm trying to understand how communication can take place with SBTM/SV over any distance, instantaneously. I think this is true from my experience. I'm separating Figure 3 (page 37) in two basic parts, comparing the circular to the linear, to show a bilevel universe that can communicate instantaneously. [*, pp. 34-35]

I will include my "Figure 3:," from my first book, here to show that we live in two realities, on one side and the other, the other half. If we could put the two parts together, then they could fit inside and overlap so that there would be nothing, as there must have been nothing before the universe was created by God.

The universe, I think, has a linear and a circular level, these two opposite bilevels make a whole. The bilevels are assembled by God to be the seen and the unseen and there is the zero point to go between the two. God must of created the zero point to allow us to communicate or connect: to our +meself,+ together to one another and to God.

Telepathy is an example of using the zero points to connect. Imagine connecting to the traders of the ES-futures market. That would be a great connection. I think this market feeling would be a channeling to other traders, since we are thinking in the same frequency. This is why "Figure 3:" [on the next part] is important because it: affirms an understanding about the zero points, shows that zero points are important to believing in SV and is highlighting the difference between linear acceleration verses angular acceleration. Acceleration is the change in velocity and this change can come about in two ways: straight and curved. Thought is like acceleration, as there is a thought in the 3D and also a corresponding thought in the 5D because our Universe is bilevel, objective and subjective, respectively.

For a thought to travel from the 5D to the R3DT, there needs to be deceleration and overlap because the 5D is at a higher frequency then down here in our realm and it happens instantaneously to transfer to the R3DT. The thought sort of needs to be translated to a lower energy when coming from the 5D to the R3DT. The R3DT frequency is spread out or broad, like linear, and is so at a lower frequency.

An alien besides a spire on the Moon.

Figure 3:

GUT: for the big and small forces in the universe

In Figure 3, the equation for the universe has a circular component, so to me this will be the frictionless harmonic oscillator as shown by equations from Figure 2 (page 23).

θ=angle of rotation
Sarc=subtended angle arc length
v=speed of light
ω=speed of rotation
rs=Planck length
•=zero point
ac=centripetal acceleration

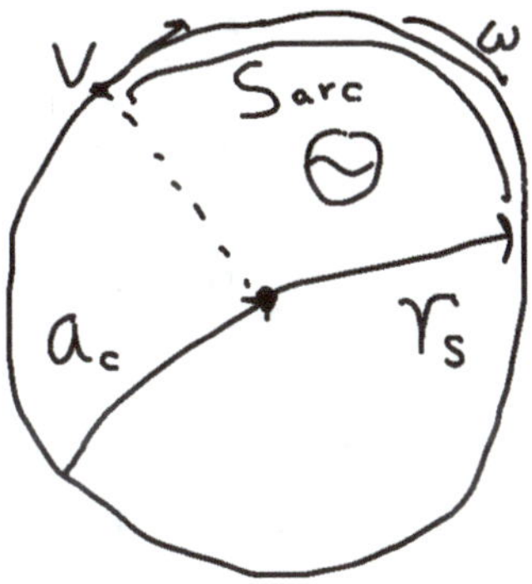

For a circular acceleration with increasing θ the constants would be: ω, ac, rs, v, rmax. Where for linear acceleration the constant would only be linear acceleration, al, because rmax and v would be increasing with time. So, given that for radians, Sarc=θ*rs and θ=Sarc /rs and ω=v /rs then v=ω*rs (equation 2) where dθ /dt=ω then ω=dSarc /dt*rs=v /rs or v=ω*rs as dSarc /dt=v

For circular acceleration, as ac increases then ω will increase as ac is proportional to ω then ac=v*ω(meter/s*rad/s) with ac=rs*ω*ω

Our Universe has dark and light masses with the dark mass as lower case m and the ordinary light Mass as capital M. The energies of the large and small must equal for the constants of our Universe to remain constant.

(Fattraction)*(distance)=1/2m vv (alternative equation 1) where, Energy Large=Energy Small
G=gravitational constant, 6.6743015x10 to the -11 (N*meter*meter/kg*kg)
G*M*m*rmax /rmax*rmax=1/2mvv
using v=ω*rs (equation 2)

$$G*M*m*rmax / rmax*rmax=1/2*m*\omega*\omega*rs*rs$$

Here the dark mass (m) will cancel from both sides giving:

$$G*M /rmax=1/2*\omega*\omega*rs*rs$$

I found from trial and error that rmax is best represented as, rmax=Z /rs

We can do an equation check by knowing the constants and the two equations we have: alternative equation 1 and equation 2. Solving for omega, ω, in equation 2 gives a constant, ω=v /rs, that equation 3 (below) must match if you solve for omega in it.

$$G*M /Z / rs=1/2\omega*\omega*rs*rs$$
$$G*M*rs /Z=1/2*\omega*\omega*rs*rs$$
$$G*M /Z=1/2*\omega*\omega*rs$$
$$G*M*2 /rs*Z=\omega*\omega$$
$$\omega=\sqrt{(G*M*2 /rs*Z)} \text{ (equation 3)}$$

ω=v /rs (equation 2, if Z=G and substitute in M)

The ω, in equation 3, is the frequency dimension’s speed.

I believe that there are two speed directions of clockwise and counterclockwise. The rotation gives the property of positive and negative charge. So if it is not rotating then there is zero charge.

M=Z*v*v /2*rs*G (equation 4)

M=v*v /2*rs (if Z=G)

The mass, M, for the universe, according to equation 4, must be constant because all of its variables are constant. When our Mass is converted to energy then dark energy is need to be converted into Mass to keep M constant. If dark mass and our Mass are constantly intermingling then dark energy is what is measured in Einstein’s equation for E=M*v*v. There might have to be a balance for Mass-to-Mass fusion reactions because fusion makes dark energy. The ratio of dark mass m and our mass M needs to be brought to equilibrium. I think, this becomes balanced by quasars, where they could put Mass into the universe and then that will be balanced for when the black holes consumes Mass.

The 5D might be the reason why fusion is different from fission. For fusion to happen the reaction needs to use other dimensions other than the R3DT. This might be a cause for concern if there are beings existing in the 5D. These aliens might try to stop or monitor our use of fusion type experimental reactions because it affects their space.

The reason why 5D is needed for fusion is because there is a higher frequency for the frequency dimension in 5D. With 5D having this frequency over the threshold of the required frequency for fusion, then this higher frequency means that there is a way for the protons and neutrons to fuse together with zero time and at a higher frequency than in the R3DT.

Since the dark mass (m) cancel out in equation of the Energy Large = Energy Small in Figure 3 above, then I will assume this mass is imaginary and not in the R3DT.

Note, I found that the total energy of the universe is

2.4988655x10 to the 68 Joules
if Z=G and the equation
E=M*v*v or E=v*v*v*v /2*rs is
used. I guess when Z=G then
matter and dark matter are
balanced in our Universe, end
of Figure 3. [*, pp. 37-39]

The purpose of explaining the GUT of the universe in the above “Figure 3:” is to show that there are zero points and also a +parallax+ and how the +parallax+ interacts with zero points. The concept of the +parallax+ brings forth the idea that there is a bilevel universe where the zero point is the only way to get to the bigger or smaller dimensions.

I think that the **+parallax+** is a real thing outside the human body. Since God created humans in his image, I believe that yes, this is because the universe would also be in the image of God, because he used his word to make it be. God is the

> word, the first and the last morphed together and this is similar to the **+parallax.+** This is as a ring, connected as a big loop's ends put together as one and twisted to make the infinity symbol, as a **+whirlwind+** in its circuit. [*, p.204]

If we want to believe that the third eye (in the pineal gland) can send and receive, then my GUT of the universe is my offer to you to have a faith that this is true and not vanity. According to the bible, our image is in God's image since God created the universe and we represent an image of God or the universe so the brain we use is a way to communicate to God and through the universe. I think this communication is represented by the pineal gland because the pineal gland is central to the brain and there is only one of them in the physical body.

Our pineal gland acts as a zero point communicator as the pineal gland is like a cloud chamber where it can send out and intercept signals from the subconscious. To be a satisfactory trader, then I think one would have to be knowledgeable at opening the third eye with an input discipline. If you can firstly control the input into the third eye then the output from your brain, in thoughts, can be trained secondarily, because firstly the inputs need to be controlled.

I would think one wants to protect their body by watching what is inputted into it and around it. I also think that self care is important and to reduce stress by eating the right foods for the body: natural foods, scrag soup for collagen; and also meditations with soul, spirit and body. One can meditate by deep breaths and mentally visualizing something. Visualize how to trade ES-futures successfully, meditate with SV and get information from your +meself+ about how to trade ES-futures. Knowing the +meself+ is possible if you can listen to SV. So nosce te ipsum, know your +meself+ in order to use your intuition to its fullest extent. As for the pineal gland, it can be calcified or ridged. [If the gland is calcified then it probably does not work as intended, so next let's learn about the decalcification process.]

Chapter 30: The purpose of having a decalcified pineal gland and the connections to the chakras

30-0 From how I understand calcification with the pineal gland, it is that the calcified pineal gland is ridged and therefore cannot secret chemicals as easily as if the pineal gland is soft and pliable. The pineal gland, that is decalcified, helps with better intuition because the pineal gland is able to see things that the other five senses don't sense as easily. The pineal gland is located in the back center of the third ventricle. Being there, the pineal gland is immersed in the cerebral spinal fluid, CSF, Figure 7. When the pineal gland is decalcified then it can input and output information.

I believe it acts as a receiver and transmitter. I have studied the pineal gland and I find that it allows for the use of unconscious abilities, one being telepathy. Having the ability to sense thoughts allows for the better understanding of SBTM/SV. This is because SBTM/SV allows for the understanding of thoughts from the unconscious. As I do BTM, voices will be heard, in part of my brain that helps to decipher the audio track that I'm listening to. Here, in the underline above, I found using SV the information of: **~Ya me hear the voices from the man at the center of it.~**

Note: I believe that ~**the man at the center of it~** is the **+meself.+** This could also be in reference to the tree of life from some stories of the Garden of Eden. In that there is at one end, the tree of life, and at the other is, the tree of knowledge. **+1st chakra+** is the tree of life and **+meself+** is the tree of knowledge. Since the **+1st chakra,+** I have found in SV, doesn't say much, but his actions are profound, this is because of Adam and Eve's original sin of eating of the apple of this double tree. In essence I believe, the **+1st chakra+** is mute and he tries to mute the **+meself+** by calcifying it, to make it separate in the brain. With a free **+meself+** then one can get better intuition.

30-1 I believe when we think in our head, there is a waveform that is established as a thought, this is in the form of energy.

Energy impulsed can interact with the part called the decalcified pineal grand by orientating the crystals inside that pineal grand to receive or send information. Since a decalcified pineal gland has more crystals to orient, then as a calcified one, it has a bigger antenna and then it can interact with the universe with more bandwidth.

It has been said that when one dies there is a dump of the chemicals from the pineal gland. This allows one's soul to be released from the body. From that umbilical cord that can be observed when we are astral traveling and when it is cut, on death, then the soul can go to source for reassessment and possibly repeating a failed life. On the other hand, for example, when I'm mad, and sense another's madness, my pineal gland will orient into a hateful pattern.

When I'm really mad or witness madness, I believe, my pineal gland will release a hate spark, as in electricity, within the conscious. I can feel this as an impulse of energy released as a little tick or feel it from observing another person I'm staring at who is going through a tantrum fit, for example. I have experienced this event with the electricity spark by observing a situation. This is a flight or fight choice and my muscles will intensify. I can feel the hate spark in my brain, probably at the pineal gland, and I can either lay into someone, observe it or defuse the energy by seeing through their false or evil thoughts that want to bring me down to their low energy vibrations. Others around me may also feel this spark if they are in tune with this unconscious communication, but I didn't ask them from my example above when this event occurred.

30-2 These vibrations can also be detected along the other connected chakras, not just in the third eye pineal gland chakra. Obviously, if the other chakras are connected that will make a larger antenna. To what extent these are used for, in SBTM/SV, I'm not entirely certain. I did SV and got the SC information that, **^The soul is not in the body but around it.^** Meaning, that the soul flows through the chakras and the soul can be a front line for any energy that enters into us. This makes sense, since the soul in the chakras can help warn the unconscious, the unconscious can warn the conscious and then finally even for others around you.

30-3 The specific diet I have is reducing processed foods and consuming more natural and organics in my diet. After first starting my pineal decalcification I decided to stop drinking milk. After I did this I could not run anymore because my knees would get sore. Later I switched to organic, low temperature pasteurization that allows the milk to maintain the healthy properties that the ultra pasteurized milk may loose. At this point I now believe that ultra pasteurization and the homogenization processes removes some healthy parts to milk and so I avoid these dairy products for the low temperature pasteurization method instead.

I also prefer to filter out the fluoride ion from the water I drink, but I can’t always do this. Because I have found in SBTM/SV that this process that we use for water processing has the fluoride ion to sanitize our public drinking water, but this also helps to cause calcification of the pineal gland, probably minimally. **~A little bit of fluoride in your system doesn't matter Math-they.~** A search on duckduckgo.com of the gentleman G. L. Waldbott will alert you about the problems with fluoride. So now I do indeed drink water in which the water bottles have no detectable fluoride. This is according to their laboratory testing of their water from the water producer’s website. [*, pp. 166-168]

Keeping the body up and healthy in a natural way is import for managing great intuition. One must love themselves and have faith that there is a connection of the flesh and spirit.

This requires a lot of work and faith to live the life to be one with everything else, in that this is important to do, by watching what you: eat, breathe, see, hear, taste and feel. The idea of watching the actions of our senses is real as we must be aware of what our senses are sensing in our surroundings and the condition of ourselves so that we can focus or have witness to the other side of reality, the 5D. If we know the present, then we can imagine the future in 5D. Imagine using the future to your advantage with ES trading.

As the time goes by we go to the future and the future for ES trading means making money. The future is money and I can think of the money in the future. If I can think of the money in the future, then I will imagine getting some of this money, here in the present. If we can control our thoughts then we can control our future circumstances, if the 5D is real. Trading ES-futures can give us freedom and make freedom.

ES-futures is so huge that not many people will care if I get some money from the ES mountain of money. By putting this thought into the +whirlwind+ then, this thought can go to the future, according to the +whirlwind+'s circuits you are accessing. The +meself+ can receive it and then manifest the details back to you in the present, as a thought experiment.

And Be Capital Safe by Making Money

The future self will be glad you are doing this thought experiment to give or make new freedom for yourself. You can make money as you will be joining up with your future self and combine into one. The logion in the "Gospel of Thomas," you are putting the two into one and moving that mountain of money. That is, I think Jesus would say, to go fishing in the ES-futures market and get money as you fish, as a fisher is like a trader, and traders want to be here, in this pile of money.

Chapter 1: Starting My Paper Trading Diary

Since I cannot trade, there is only about $975 in my account, I decided to do paper trading to figure out the best technique to try when I do refund my trading account. Below are some days in a month that I examined just trading in the morning, go to work and hopefully come home to my trading system and see some money made.

20240923: I see that ES could go up as it is up premarket, up 9 at 5771, around 5:00 a.m. and my intuition feels like it is an up day. After this I did SV, according to my rule (2) on page 52 and then my +Meself+ said, **~If you short you are stupid, it's going up Matthew.~** How far up? Looking at the chart, it could go up 10 points to the overnight support. So every 10 up would be $500 profit from buying one lot, that would be a pleasant paycheck each day.

I made another SV after typing the last paragraph and I get +centimeter:+ **~That thing might have to go down before it goes up.~** or one in a hundred odds it just goes up. If I put a stop in at 5765 then this would cut my losses at this point level or a negative $300. I could put in a sell limit at 5781 to sell my lot for a $500 profit. That way I could just go to work and hopefully after the open my limit would be exceeded and I would be happy when I get home.

Well I got home and ES went below

5764 and went up to 5784. So I was right that it was going up, but was cheap on my stop. I should of put a stop at 5760. So not being here to monitor the trade was dangerous, I could of changed the stop then. Either I need to stay home and monitor the trade or allow for a bigger loss by making a farther away stop. If I go to work and leave the trade, my +Meself+ would probably say (as it has been said before), **~If you snooze you loose.~**

From the above SVed, after I made my trade, I did get +centimeter,+ a +Subconscious-Metaphor+ (+S-M+) message. This was a powerful signal that something was wrong. The ES-futures chart essentially went sideways today, and I should of gotten out of my trade or reduced my limit to about $100 or increased my stop, for a bigger stop loss.

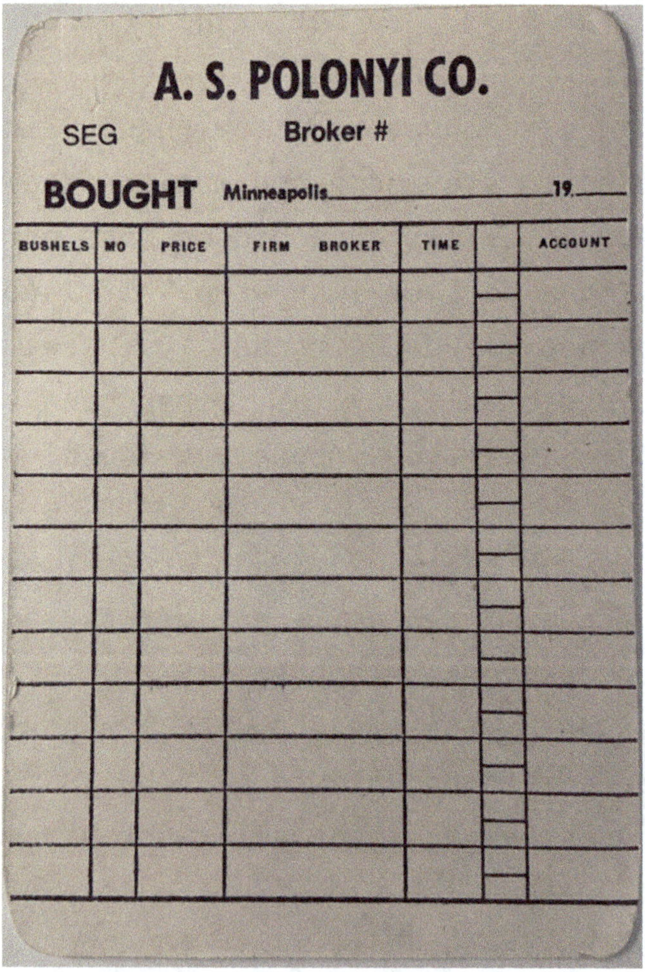

A. S. POLONYI CO.

SEG Broker #

BOUGHT Minneapolis ________________ 19____

BUSHELS	MO	PRICE	FIRM BROKER	TIME		ACCOUNT

ES Trading Worksheet for a Day Trade	
Date	September 23, 2024
Time	5 a.m.
Instrument	ESZ24
Start Action	BUY at 5771
Stop	5765
Limit	5781
Pattern Detected	Down to 5764 then up
End Action	Went through stop
Overview	Need deeper stop
Profit made	**Negative $300**

20240926: I just saved my manuscript file to another name and lost the last two days of text, or a couple of pages! Well I'm listening to the SV for this morning and I just got that message, **~Say-tin is going to try to stop you, you better be careful Matthew.~** However I lost paper money two days and made money yesterday, so I'm down about negative $850. I heard on the news that the Budget Crisis was forgone till the next time as the US Government is funding itself and I think ES-futures is going up.

In the Economic Calendar there are the Jobs and GDP reports today and I feel that they are going to be great. So I remember at 5:10 a.m. I bought ESZ24 (I should put the "instrument" of exactly what I'm buying) at 5824 with a sell limit at 5833 and a stop at 5814. We will see what happens when I get back from work.

Before the mistake in saving my file I was making a sentence on how +Say-tin+ controls the world with money. If there was no money then we would not be feeding him. When I got home my stop was not blown, the market went to 5819 (I had it at 5814) but it went up to 5830 so I did not have a chance with my trade today, because my sell was at 5833.

Next morning I'm editing my book and I noticed my stop was not crossed and the limit was not made so this means my trade was still live. My broker requires about $12,000 to keep it overnight so it was probably liquidated before 4:00 p.m., I still lost money.

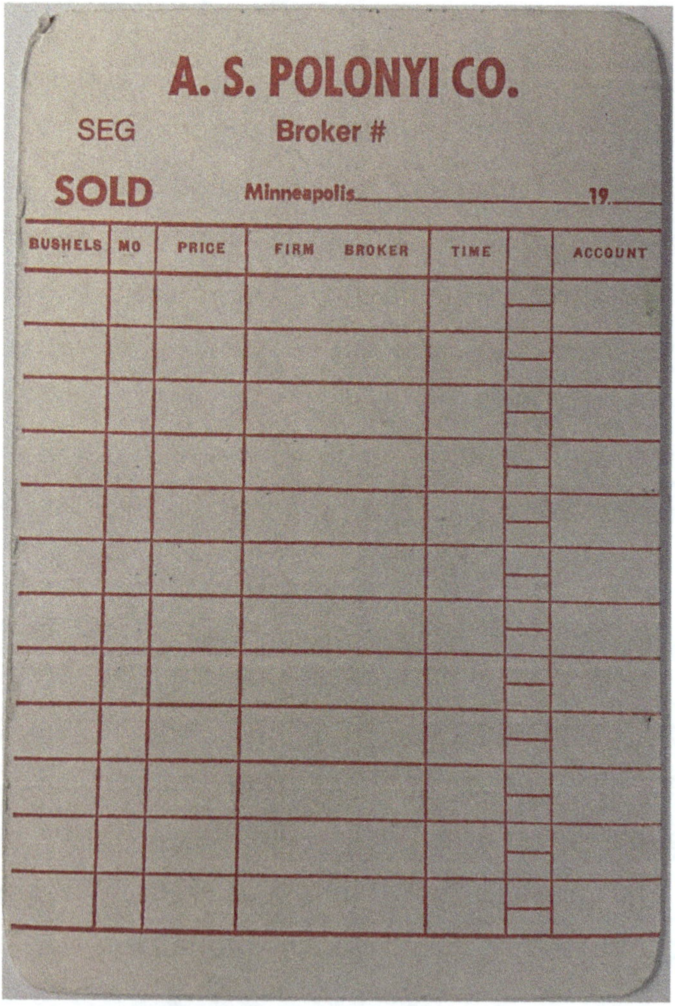

A. S. POLONYI CO.

SEG Broker #

SOLD Minneapolis ________ 19__

BUSHELS	MO	PRICE	FIRM BROKER	TIME		ACCOUNT

ES Trading Worksheet for a Day Trade	
Date	September 26, 2024
Time	5:10 a.m.
Instrument	ESZ24
Start Action	BUY at 5824
Stop	5814
Limit	5833
Pattern Detected	Down then up, but did not cross my limit so this trade is still live. At 3:45 p.m. this trade would of probably been liquidated by my broker because I didn't have the margin for overnight trading.
End Action	liquidated
Overview	Need lower limit
Profit made	**Negative probably $500**

The way I'm trading is not the right way with just $5000. I need to monitor my trade with the money I have and just make $200 because it is as gambling to hold it longer. So if someone says I'm gambling by trading ES they don't know my rules, it should not be gambling if I just get $200 and make myself done for the day.

Once again, yesterday was ruff for me. When I was walking in the evil neighborhood, I walked by a city bus stop and smelt some lingering smoldering smoke. It was from someone that recently was getting high on percocet or some drug (probably mixed with fentanyl) burned in aluminum foil. I smelled this third hand smoke and my symptoms were a light head in my forebrain and then pins pricking my lips, as if that they were big. So I think this is +Say-tin+ guiding me to this hazardous waste of the city bus stop to make me have a needy mind.

Now with that off my chest, I will continue to get the city bus to my school bus stop, but just wait in the safe area I know of by my school bus stop. I don’t want to wander in the evil +kan-de-land+ neighborhood and get myself into trouble. I don’t want to ride my bicycle there or even my car, as I think bad things will happen to them. I got sleep last night, as I want to go to bed at an undeviating time, not some discursive times to mess up my circadian clock. I need to have quiet sleep to trade ES.

Now back to trading. From what I

remember from my trading before, I could make money. Then after I made money I would try to get out on a limb and look for more risky trades to make more money, to be macho. That is the fatal flaw in trading ES-futures, trying to change your rules with your ego. My rules will work as I have a realization now, with a certain price point, from $12.50 on duff days to $600 on inspirational moments. So why not keep that ratio, basically make a maximum of about 10% per trading session and then, just one trade, call it quits for the day. This means, if I have $5000 in my trading account then, get out after I make a trade and profit $500. Now, if I lose, then I'll need a stop to get me out for safety.

My Dad said something like, "Your

first loss is your best loss." Meaning that if I loose again, it will be worse, a downward spiral. So I need to take my time to find the right trade for the rules I trade by. That is the reason to paper trade and to get your rules set for the amount of money you will be risking. Using rules can take the bad emotion out of trading.

The experienced trader will likely have rules and not cross those rules. One thing rules should stop is trading too fast, so one needs a strong and fresh, not a gripple mind, so one will not gamble their money away. My old Rule number two, (2), failed and I revised it to my current Rules on pages 53 to 54. It takes rules and intuition to effectively trade and make money.

The last time I traded I thought I could get my money back, but traded the opposite 90% of the time and got left with about $1000. However, this time I did not close my account, one month there was almost $18 ($15 for an inactive account and $2.20 for CME market data, real time quotes) taken to maintain it, but still having my account open gives me pause to figure this out, for my situation.

Alright, my paper trading chapter is over, because I lost too much paper money. I did not have big enough of a stop or too big a limit. Since I'm at work it would be high risk that I get the market direction right. On the other hand if I could have a lower limit then it might work, as long as the stop or limit would take me out of the market sooner, since I can't trade past 3:45 p.m. with $5000 in my account. I will never make my real money back trading with big goals of money gains with just $5000 in my account, as I have year after year. This might be happening to me for a reason. So let's discuss another analysis of ES-futures and look at being consistent by following the rules. I need to just take my time.

The next two pages have trading logs so that one can: know what they are doing; be able to look back and try to self-correct, if they need to become a better trader; or need to look hard and refund their account.

Chapter 2: Examining the Trends of ES-Futures

My Dad would show me a 30-years Bond chart and cover the second half for me to predict where the left side chart would be going. As I would predict, then my Dad would pull the chart to the left some more to predict and show the next support or bottom and top in the chart. This technical analysis told me that the markets have a language and mood. There are always buyers and sellers and this will move markets by definition. So one skill an ES trader has is the ability to watch the market move in a chart. I think of the market as an organism or neighborhood that has a mood. I want to telepathically connect to this beast to see which way it will go.

One time I told my Dad that trading ES-futures is like waiting for an animal to be downed in an attack from another animal, as what happens in Africa with a lion and a wildebeest. This story compares money to meat as in, I can be early and get some meat when the lion is busy chewing, but before the other scavengers get there. My Dad's response to that was "No," that is not correct. Well I still see the similarity though, to real life in the market. I would be like a little bug that could go down and fly in and bite off some meat, small and unnoticed or fly out with a stop if I am noticed. So, if I could get out with $1000 worth of meat to safety then I would be feeling great. However, if I fly in and get in the area when the lion takes a bite of the meat <u>then I would die in</u>

the stomach of the lion.

In the above SV I found: **~If you happen to get stuck in the stomach of a lion, I don't care Matthew.~** Getting in and out requires timing when trading the ES-futures market. I just can't say, "I'm going in and something great will happen.," I need to time it to what the market is doing and wait for the beast to fall, then go in and take the behoof. If I'm going to take advantage in the ES-futures market then I will have to wait and read the market, by taking my time. This was my biggest error, just going into the market, continuously, and not appreciating the dangers of getting out of the market.

I did make money with +reverse

speech+ before, but I got sloppy by thinking I graduated to a higher level and could handle it now, wrong! I need to get back to basics and watch more than trade, to be a great trader. I need to be able to see when the trade is mostly noise verses when a market shift makes an opportunity for me.

Often ES will go way up, or to turbo jet up and then back down, or vice versa, so it would go down then pop up, then back to a support, for example. These are gleeful times to trade, in my opinion. If I can think where I would trade, if I had $50,000 instead of $5,000, then since I just have $5,000 I can wait to watch the market instead of trading right away. I can take my time, and watch for my entry level.

If I see that ES has to go up today, then just wait for ES to go down. I will be thinking, *ES is going down, but I will buy it when it starts to show going up. No way, ES is going down. Then wow. This is impossible, ES just dropped and the market is crazy.* There is no news for ES to do this.

When ES really moves then some hedge fund just probably sold a lot of contracts. Now it would be a nice time to buy, because ES, as I feel ES, has to cycle back up as it is contrary now to reality. I think this is how I want to trade now, in my situation like this, with the size of my account. I want to see the trend reversals and try to wait for the bottom or top. Once I can take my time I can trade and get out after $200 to $2000, this gives me a freedom to success.

I remember when I visited the Minneapolis Grain Exchange with my Dad, about 1987, and I was there because it was, Take Your Child to Work Day. My Dad had a section of a work cubical on the floor of this exchange and there were mostly men and some women working and some even making trades with open outcry at the pit, in the corner of the big room. My Dad had a way to chart the 30-year Bond market on graph paper as he watched the big boards on the big wall nearby. After the market opened I looked around and saw one man watching very closely one of the big boards, with real time quotes on it. Whenever I would glance over to him he was staring intently for something. Today

I think he was just waiting for the top or bottom and getting ready to trade if the situation unfolded in the market that, then would allow him to make a trade. To me this was a conservative trader and he was trying to think with the market and follow his rules. This trader was, melancholy, looking for a signal to move and trade in the market, but had to have a signal first. Just looking at the ticks in the market helps me to gather information on the mood of the market.

If I can just have some patience and wait for the big moves in the market and then maybe I can make some money. Like the floor trader at the Minneapolis Grain Exchange, I saw way back, I too should just watch the market to see its mood and try to see the bottom or top and then know with my intuition where it is going and make my trade with my rules.

There are rules for me and there must be rules for the market. One natural law for the ES-futures market is that not one entity can control ES for very long. There is a point when the control moves over to a different set of traders. One could say a freedom to trade is in someone's else hands.

The freedom to trade is a real concept, it is a natural law to trading. If someone has money to trade they supposedly want to make money. If the trader doesn't make money then that trader lost the freedom to trade.

This freedom to trade is similar to human rights of natural law, where one has a written law and an unwritten law to live by. If I get hurt in the evil neighborhood, then I will not want to go back there. I can't sustain myself in the evil neighborhood very long, I'll get hurt or nocent. I'll have to stay in a better neighborhood in order to recover myself to my own healthy self. In essence I gave my freedom to go in the evil neighborhood to someone else, because I'm not going back there. Now, there might be a set amount of freedom to go around.

Rev. Dr. Martin Luther King Jr. tried to make new freedom for the perpetual slavery of the first African-Americans. African people were brought here and put into total slavery and they had trouble leaving. Today in America, we still call this heritage of people enslaved from Africa as African-Americans because we should remember the horror of their life, when the original African-Americans came to the “New World,” I think into chattel slavery and the culture they have to this day as really, African-American. I see the term, African-American, as a metaphor of the evil that they went through and continues to go through in the USA because of systemic racism.

How to get out of slavery and the system of the evil neighborhood is to make freedom. If someone has more freedom and others don’t, then that could make everyone bitter. We should love our neighbors, as in the bible, and love God with all our heart, soul and mind. God has everlasting freedom, a freedom that can multiply a hundred or more times. If people are ready to be free, then they can express themselves with what they: need or want, get upset with or get happy with.

We need to communicate to find the answer to what are people's boundaries so we can live together. First we need to love God to get this extra freedom of living together, otherwise there will be only a set amount of freedom, even with a greater population. Evil would have to be casted out, as much as humanly possible, we are stronger together. Evil just wants a set amount of freedom or even less! Someone who has freedom to trade ES has a life, just as someone has freedom to live in a better neighborhood.

It is said that there is Life, Liberty and the pursuit of Happiness (TPH). Liberty is just another name for freedom and the TPH is just another way to say love God with all my heart, soul and mind. Because our souls have a road map and God has a destination for us to go in. One's life is lost if they lose freedom or TPH. We need all three: life, freedom and TPH to be successful in life. It is said, to find a need and provide for it to be successful. Well, I say that to find a need and fill it by being successful will then be creating more freedom for others. If you find yourself in the evil neighborhood then this is like a message from your soul and even God to make a new path to freedom.

The ES-futures market can go into

an evil spot, then the good will try to make new freedom by taking away evil and making new money. ES has to make new money, because of inflation and the eventual worthlessness nature of dollar bills. No one would use a dollar bill from one hundred years ago for today. They would be better off selling it to a dollar bill collector. ES could be thought of getting hurt by going into the evil neighborhood as a dip in points. When traders get out because they are loosing money, then those traders who see an opportunity to help and have the means to trade according to their rules, will make money.

The market has everything blended together from the USA and even the world, because it is one unified market, from technology. Those who invested in the evil neighborhood and did not know it are then given the message, “This hurts here in this evil neighborhood, I’m leaving, because I see truly what it is.” While in the same ES market other traders are getting a bargain buy, better cornerstone and are better off, to a point (no pun intended). They see the +net-scape+ because they will be making money by buying off of the bottom and now it’s going sideways, making a horizon’s landscape, and then the lumpen will make money when it goes up. Even for those better off, the market has its cycles, where they get out of from the better neighborhood. If affluent people leave a neighborhood, then, when or if that happens, they think it will go bad from their instinct.

Chapter 3: ~ES is run by Say-tin.~

If I just trade consciously my ES trade could go to negative because even if I find a pattern, ES can try to circle back and go against my trade. I would be trading with blinders on, not seeing the whole situation. As my example of paper trading shows, I was trying to trade with $5000 and then go to work leaving it trade by itself with me hoping that my trade would try to cross my limit, to make my money. This experiment showed, that testing with paper money was not a bad strategy, but I needed better rules to succeed with real money.

A better strategy would be to ask my +Meself+ to guide me to trade and then watch the trade. (Perhaps, now with my current rules on page 53, I just start my trade on intuition.) I need to watch the trade because I will only have $5000 in my account and this small amount is only safe to day trade ES-futures once and then, for me, get out for the rest of the day. The difference is defeating +Say-tin+ by taking my time and listening to my +Meself.+

+Say-tin+ is what seeps into my thoughts with idle thinking, because there is sin everywhere in this world. Our World is fallen and has a dense frequency that transforms our Godly image into a corrupted image. Adam and Eve ate of the tree of Knowledge and the Life. Knowledge of good and evil is what they got. Once they had this knowledge, someone probably said, “They should die.” Because Adam and Eve had a +parallax+ then, they had to discern nice and bad, now it was not just good, but evil too, everywhere. Evidently evil was only at the tree of Knowledge and the Life, in the Garden of Eden.

Instead of life they got death by getting the knowledge of sin, which leads to death, because this sin knowledge is of the bad, and is death. Once someone has knowledge, how do they use it shows the knowledge of understanding, as they now need to show the need to get experience on how to live with this new knowledge. Adam and Eve needed a new time to take, to try to understand what was happening to them and choose which way to choose, which required them to die because their life was in the Garden of Eden a place without linear time, but circular time. In that understanding good and evil required knowledge of linear time. I believe that the higher self is in the higher realm with circular time and we can communicate with it through SV.

Communicating with one's higher-spirit allows for the life to reenter our body, through a new life. This is what makes us as humans, more powerful than +Say-tin+ because we can have our +meself+ go to the 5D, above this Earth plane. This is the reason why we cannot successfully trade ES without having help from above, in our life. Our body can die, but our spirit is of God, from his breath, image and God's Holy spirit, the eternal and good.

To block +Say-tin+ in life requires knowing what bad knowledge is and also what bad life is. Healthy life is freedom, while +Say-tin+ is death. Just sitting idly by will be inviting +Say-tin+ into your spirit to cause you harm. One must call on Jesus to help cast out +Say-tin+ from your field or bubble around you. Open your voice box, ~+“Jesus help. +Say-tin+ get out.”+~ Knowledge can interest you and entice you to spend time in some other endeavor or live in a different place, a better place. To live the straight life and not crooked lives as with the +parallax+ and doing the opposite.

As we know from my explanation of the evil neighborhood, freedom can be lost, similar to how money is lost trading ES the wrong way, the opposite. Knowledge can try to hide what it is, because there is enduring knowledge, or truth, and bad knowledge or vanity. Vanity is as a covering up of something that does change, to make it look truthful or new and ongoing and not changing.

Vanity is a covering up like make-up, to show something as not changing when it does change. If something is obviously being covered up, but shown through, then that person that is saying or doing this is vain. Something not true is vanity because it is not going to happen in reality. Vanity of vanity is the covering up of something twice. The equations of vanity of vanity are: Bad (multiplied by) Vanity = Good and also there is

Good (multiplied by) Vanity = Bad.

A real world example of vanity is, there is a requirement to repair your home and you are going through your insurance company. Someone recommends a contractor to repair your home and when the insurance company comes for the estimate the contractor is there while the estimator is at work doing the estimation of damage.

The contractor is basically going to get paid by using the insurance payment for the lost property. That is nice, but this is a corrupted system. Money leads to corruption. After the estimate there might be some back and fourth between the contractor and the insurance company. The contractor is handling it for you with the insurance company.

You as a homeowner is now out of the negotiating because the contractor is handling the money issues. After the money is set, then the contractor will come to your home and have you sign a contract. Now it is the choice of the homeowner if they are willing to spend more money, if the contractor can't finish with the payment from the insurance company.

The contractor may not do all that they say. The contractor might do each home like a form, to fit it to each situation, as that is easier and less risky for the contractor. However, the homeowner might feel left in the cold when the renovation or work is completed. The contract that the homeowner signed is a fillable form, they negotiated nothing, it is just fill-in-the-box and leave. Their particular situation is glanced over and approximated to the general situation for the contractor, so his workers can do the job efficiently. The homeowner has a bad impression of the contractor because of the money involved and the quality of the work. A smaller company could of done better, if they wanted to impress the homeowner. That is why they say, shop around. The job might not even be necessary to repair, it is just vanity. You are convinced by vanity of vanity from the contractor's nice words and did it anyway, now you are sore as you see your mistake.

If someone has words of baiting to

get someone to do something then the situation changes and this is as they call it, “a bait and switch.” This is vanity of vanity, changing one thing for the other. It should have been sufficient, but there was greed involved and in reality it was bad.

I’ve done this vanity switch myself with my apartment roommate when I made a roommates’ agreement, then I seemed to change the terms to suit me. We should all love our neighbors. As a love from above, in heaven, as a family love for each other. There is a different love up there in heaven. Even for someone bad, I cannot change their behavior, just love them for who they are, and stay away if I feel uncomfortable.

Vanity of vanity is something good that changes to bad or something bad and changed to better. It is like this is a good price to go up, for ES, but it looks good and will be shortly bad. This is a +parallax+ where just the opposite is selected. To see through the vanity of vanity one needs to take their time and discern and also use their +meself+ for a trouvaille of an opinion or secret. They need to get rid of or get away from the evil salesman called +Say-tin+ and ask Jesus for help.

Before I wrote the above chapter I did an SV that I was listening to many times. What I found was: **~Matt there are some spirits around and they can coalesce to harm ye.~ ~Matt if you trade by yourself you are screwed.~**

~See that Say-tin uses fear.~ ~One says the good, if you listen to the others you will have a bad day, please don't gamble.~

The stars will rotate according to the Earth's axis and axial precession, as you can see at night. Things will rise and set at the horizon. If I were to claim that the Sun will not rise, that is vanity. The Sun will rise and set, I would be vain to truly say that. The weather caused by the Sun is not vanity, because that weather is chaos and will do something different each time we can think, as a butterfly flaps its wings something will happen that we cannot vaticinate from the time before. So take your time with the Sun rise and set and not the flapping a butterfly's wings, to be a living ES trader.

Chapter 4: Linear Programming of ES-Futures Trading

I need to do a feasibility graph of my ES-futures trading. This would make a Feasibility Region (FR) that I can find, to relatively safely trade in, compared to the risky trades I have done and lost. The FR can be used to graph a two dimensional region in the 2D-plane, that inputs all of your skills and the understandings of the market you are trading in onto the Y-axis and then the amount of money on the X-axis. So one must stay in the FR to keep their money and hopefully make more, as drifting outside of this FR is to loose money. In the FR there should be a sweet point to make the most money for each trade, if it is completed by the rules and intuition.

Why did I lose my money...?, I think it was because I got to a decision to trade too quickly and didn’t follow my rules. Trading quickly is like gambling, without a palladium! Even with safeguards, if I’m consistent to trade once a day and use the stop and limit, I will still fail because I found worse and still worse trades to get into which resulted in a downward spiral, given less risk money each trade. So I could start out making money and then let down my guard and think I can trade every day consistently and additionally also think I’m so wise and pretentious so that I could trade in harder and harder trading environments, but this resulted in losing trades, so I needed to refund my futures brokerage account.

Even when I refunded my trading account I would want to keep a bad trade to try and ride it out because I think I'm right. This made large losses that I was not able to recover from because there was a psychological aspect that I felt I could only lose money. Eventually, I thought about what I was doing, I came to my truth that it was me making the wrong trades and I needed to remedy the situation and trade in a different way. I like to pray during my trade if it goes bad.

Praying while listening to SV gives me confidence in my trade as I identify the false information and correct information. The correct information will come from the intuition as long as my body is clean from toxic chemicals that would make my brain become needy and cloudy thinking. Even if I know the intuition I might of traded early and have to wait for the market to go in my direction. This is a waiting game so I like to listen to my SV to pass the time and root myself up with play-by-play action. From this SV I get different ideas that might explain the ES-future market and indicate where it is going. If the percentage of positive SV ideas outweigh the negative then I can rest assured that I made the right trade. If I just wait then I can find a market reaction that will indicate future market movement.

The market for trading ES-futures can show extremes that are convenient places to trade in and bad, given a certain experience level and rules.

When you have an understanding for a market along with your intuition of which way the market will go, then you can just wait for the setup and make a trade. Your trade, if you wait for a setup and sedulous with your rules, then this is not gambling when you see the pattern and act on it. The next figure is basic algebra of the 2D-plane.

Here are some basic rules for the 2D-plane, with the concept of the straight line and its equation of: y=(slope)*x+(y-intercept). The slope is the rise divided by the run and the y-intercept is just where the line crosses the Y-axis. For example in the Graphing Basics there is a red dotted line for y=(5/8)x-6 going through the fourth quadrant.

Graphing Basics

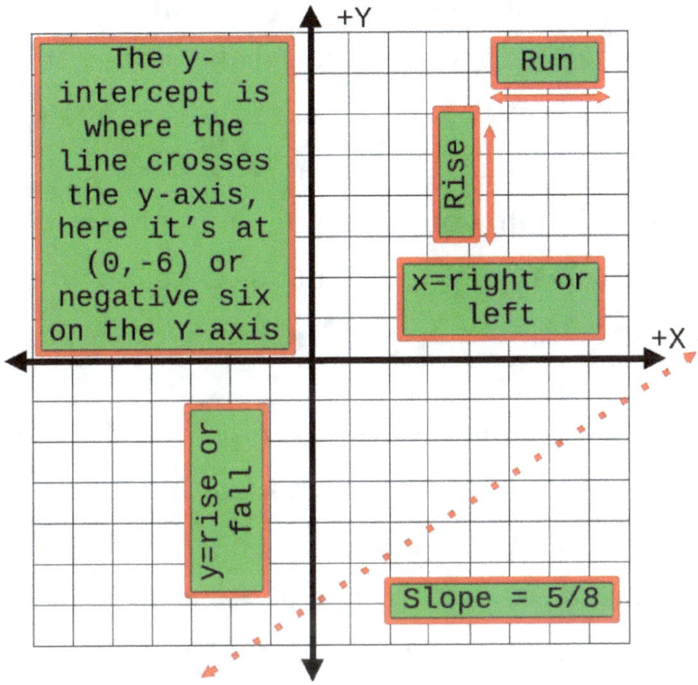

We can graph a trade onto the 2D-plane that is safe to keep and make money. The safe area to trade is in the upper right hand quadrant of this graph, the first quadrant.

And Be Capital Safe by Making Money

When you start a trade you are at zero dollars profit, but when, and if you make a profit, you make money then you are moving to the right, along the positive X-axis. When you make a profit then you can get out of the market by making a round trip in your trade.

The round trip is getting in and then getting out of the market along a trade segment, because there always needs to be a buyer and a seller and so you have to complete the round trip to make money. On an (x,y)-graph plane, the X-axis could be the money gained in a trade. We need to identify labels for the X and Y axes.

The X-axis would be for any set amount of money made that trading day. A negative amount of money would drag a trading line into the second quadrant, or the negative X-axis. This would be bad, as this person's account would be depleting. They would either have to withdrawal the remaining amount or refund the account to the initial trading requirement's value. We want to watch making bad trades and going negative in the trading account. One way to stop bad trades is just trade once a trading day.

Another way to stop a bad trade is to know at what point level to place the stop and then actually let it stop the trade if the market gets down to it. Having trading experience can allow one to place the stop correctly, at a support, know when to get out of the trade. This information can be displayed onto a 2D graph.

Graphic to help understand the concept of the FR.

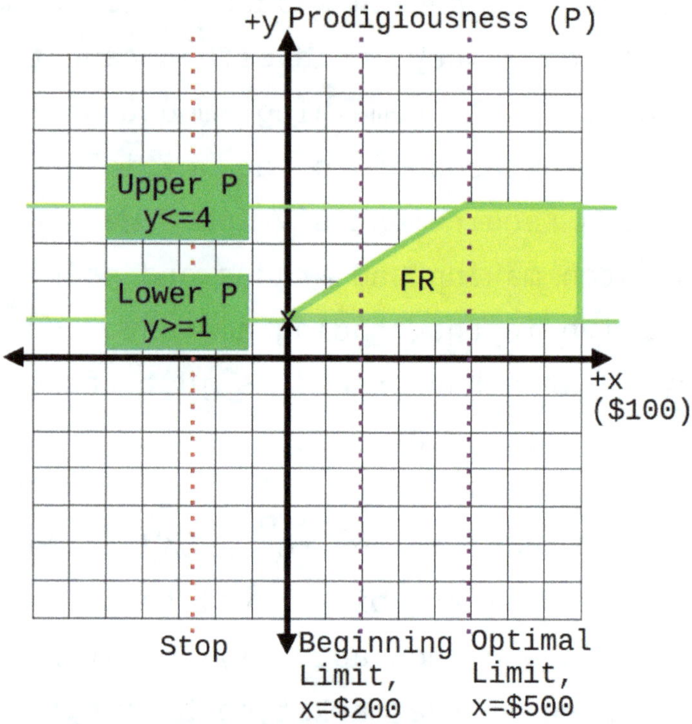

X, as the y-intercept, the trade start

The above representation and the Graphing Basics, are two dimensional graphs that can show a relationship between the X-axis and the Y-axis. The trade line has two components: the slope multiplied by the x-variable and the y-intercept added to it.

For our purposes here, this graph can be used to show the amount of money made in a day along the X-axis, if two things happen: the trader was following the rules, represented by the y-intercept coordinate (0,y) to enter into a trade and then the ability to understand the market, as represented by the slope to get out of the trade.

For me, with one FR, we have to force one trade a day, by default. Because from my experience, it must be over my head to trade more than once a trading day. So, for all linear programming in this book, there needs to be only one trade a day allowed.

This is a constraint on my trading: less than or equal to one (trade<=1).

With the one-day-a-trade, this will keep the number of FRs to one. I suppose if the market recrudesces itself and makes a channel, the FRs could overlap if the same situation repeats itself, a so-called wash and repeat. This is where a pattern repeats itself and a nice place to make money, as the trader sees this setup, just entering and exiting a trade at the boundaries of the channel. These setups can be documented onto a FR to be used when the pattern repeats in the future.

For a FR on the 2D plane there are two basic concepts: making money on the X-axis for amount of money; and on the

Y-axis, this can now be used for getting into a trade by following the successful trading rules gained from trading knowledge and using understanding from one’s intuition to get out of this trade. Starting up on the Y-axis (or x=0), above zero from the origin, can be interpreted as using better trading technique and money making potential because of following rules or using skills, is with y>=1.

The rules are important to follow for entering into a trade. Not following the rules leads to a loss of money from carelessness. One must use wisdom besides the rules to really, consistently, make money trading ES-futures. Using the rules gives a FR some borders or constraints to trade in, one is defined as y>=1, if, the trader used the rules. Besides using the rules, symbolized as where the trading line starts above the X-axis, there is also the understanding of the intuition of the trader, himself or herself, some skills.

The trading Y-axis Proficiency, (P), is the rise and the X-axis movement would be the run, the money. So that the positive slope equation is where there is in the success in using intuition P that is divided by X. So our formula here would include change, as in a slope. The slope is P divided by X, to give P/X. The slope put into the slope-intercept formula is shown as, y=(P/X)*x+(y-intercept). The P that is small (1 to 3) has a potential to make a lot of money. With a small slope, less than one, this gives a shallow line, it is close to horizontal. If P is small, this has a meaning that the X would be even larger (measured in $100 increments) to make a shallow line for the top segment of the FR. If an expert trader has a P of 1 then the X would be in proportion as larger, about $5000. This would give a slope of 1/5000, meaning that $5000 is made in the trade with just a P of one. A novice trader may have a P of 10, but their X is only $500, giving them a slope of 1/$50. A novice needs to quick get a profit, with a limit set, or risk losing the money by letting a bad trade run with a P of zero.

Overall the best traders will have more money and time for their trade to mature beating the random cycle of ups and downs in the market churning. For example, ES-futures at the opening bell is labile, as the market can have a lot of buyers and then the next five seconds have a lot of sellers as it zigzags up or down.

All trades have an entry and exit. The Y-axis intercept can be a start or entry into the trade point and the vertical rise per run from there the exit, for example: I buy one lot using my rules, then my FR has a P of 5 to 10 over a X of $100 to about $1000, are used for the slope in the trade, then I can exit and profit at a limit by the critical point, or top of the FR. The rise over run, from the y-intercept, is to be a measuring of a prodigiousness or P/X for a trade in the market. Then up the Y-axes would be thought of as an increasing of the probability of successfully using one's skills with the trade made per trading session within a FR. Some days there could be no money made and that would be an infinite slope or vertical line. Where a more horizontal line means that this slope can make more money verses a more vertical one if the trade gets to the limit, and the trade is complete. It is better to get out with a profit then to hold the trade because it has to go the other way, making you lose money, in order to continue to a greater profit for the next run in your direction. Because of the randomness of the ES-futures market, it might be best not to trade some days when you feel off or tired.

If there were no trades then the trade line would not matter, as the trader could survive to trade a better day. As the slope with zero money is a vertical line. If there is a trade in a trading session, then the y-equation (trade line) would show potentially how much money could be made along the X-axis, however there are other constraints that will make a FR to shorten the trade line. For example, the trade line equation could be y<=(1P/$100)*x+1P, because there is basic probability of the trader being up to a P/X of (1/$100) with rules at a skill level of one. To my estimation, a P/X of 0.01 is better than a 50-50% chance for gambling with a P of zero. Someone trading in a gambling way would then for this day, have a y-intercept of zero or a P of zero and they should not trade, a horizontal line, madness.

If the P is zero then this would draw a horizontal line on the two dimensional plane through the y-intercept. By definition a horizontal line is an even chance that the market could tick up or down, like a flip of a coin, this is gambling. A horizontal P line through the origin (0,0) and also having a zero slope, by definition, is gambling. If this trade makes money then it is just by chance because it is not in the money making area of the graph for a trader's FR. The money making area is bordered by constraints that put the trade into a FR. Some work has to be put into where the FR is at, in order to be relatively sure one will make money in their trade, so all valid investments in ES-futures needs a nonzero positive slope. Once we have the P for our ES trading factory we need a placement on the Y-axis by using a y-intercept.

A line has a slope and a y-intercept, as in the “slope-intercept formula” for a line, gives a start point for a trade. The y-intercept, I think of as, a place to start for the ES trader and make a trade. If the trader is not using rules, then that is bad and they should have a y-intercept of zero as a start point. For an experienced wealthy trader (has risk money of more than $20,000) then, I would use a y-intercept of one to five. For a small account that would make trading more complicated or risky, they would need ten or more rules. Each rule could be one digit on the Y-axis for about ten rules as this is probably the most you would need. Now we have a

P line for making the top part of our quadrilateral or trapezoid shaped FR to make money in and know how we are making this money.

Our P line equation gives us some trading line options for the best the trader can hope for, on average, if the rules are followed and they have trading with understanding of when to get out of the trade. The P lines are rarely horizontal. Now we need more constraints that are vertical and add the trade line, to make a quadrilateral or trapezoidal area, for showing the FR of our graph, to know where to make money and get out of the market.

One constraint would be greater then or equal, to say $100 payday or greater. This equation could be set as, x>=$100. Here, in this trade I could just scalp $100 and get out of the market and this market could go up then go down and back up to $100, like a roller coaster. If the trader aims low, their trade might be like a roller coaster, so that after this excitement the trader just gets out with $100 and quit all-day, x=$100 as a dotted line.

You can have better trades if you watch for the setup and not just look for the first trade when you login to your trading platform, as was likely done for the last paragraph. Here, we can add the intuition in to make a shallow slope, up the graph and making money along the positive X-axis and a set value for the y-intercept, with rules. For me to follow my rules I have a goal to put my y-intercept at one and a limit with x>=$1000, >= is a solid line. To trade with a mini-ES and a $100 limit is not worth the risk that the trader goes into the market with their risk money, they are a novice trader if they do that, they should find more money by waiting for safer trades that go with the market and are way bigger than a $100 profit.

My novice rules were [please see page 52 for my old rules and pages 53 and 54 for my current rules] looking safe but I did SV before the trade and I looked for a over $100 per day opportunity. Now I (I might need to) do SV only after the trade to consult my +Meself+ to see what it says and then stay in or get out if you feel something is wrong with the trade to be capital safe with the $100. My chances are low if I continue with trades like $100, but now I think knowing about the: +parallax+ problem, support levels and taking my time to see the trade can help me become a Professional Trader as indicated in my Table 1. I think it's in the ballpark to help you plan on becoming an ES-futures trader if you have the will and the need to be free.

Table 1 has the basic components of the futures trader. It all comes down to if the futures trader is early, on time or late. I can be early and after I move my stop into the money for safety, then the market will see my stop and get it. I need to not be too early to see where the market is going, to speculate what it has to do before my chart setup. With this done, then I can trade on time and make money.

Table 1: Types of ES-Futures Traders				
Name	Beginner	Novice	Expert	Professional
% Gravitate to	80	10	9	1
# Rules They Think They Need	1 to 5	5 to 10	10 to 5	5 to 1
Intuition Ability	cloudy	Insightful	clear	Laser beam
Trades in FR or Use Rules	No	No	Yes	Yes
Quits Trading	Yes	Yes	No	No
Capital Safe and Made Money	No	No	No	Yes

In the graph below is my FR where it is safest to make money. The y-intercept is just one so this trader knows how to trade and has a lot of money, but currently they need to: follow all of their rules, use their trading instinct to get into the trade, use their +meself+ to look for getting out of the trade, watch the ES chart and watch the Economic Report. Those pieces of information gives them a P of one, with a maximum of two for their large amount of risk money. Now say they enter the trade, then they will have another set of risks, to get out of the trade. It is hard to know when to get out of the trade. The +meself+ might be a valuable source of information on knowing when to safely bail out. I've traded and made $700 just to loose it as I slowly watched the money go away, I was using a small amount of risk money (less than $5000). As they say, "If you snooze, you loose." and I don't want to risk the money I made. There are always other battles the next day. I might need to know how to read the markets better or deposit more money into my account to handle more risk.

If you think of it, someone might have only $5000 in their account. If they make $500, then that would be a 10% profit. It would be just risky to trade again in the same market. Next day the market could be different and clear thinking could win the battle. How to make this 10% profit is key, because if you start out and it just happens then you cannot repeat this result again and might loose your money the next time. That would be a negative slope into loosing money on the negative-x side of the X-axis. If the best I think I can do a day is about $500 a trade, then this could give me two more constraints of a second y-limit for when the trader’s rules run into trouble, up at the y=trouble level, and the y-intercept of the trade’s start or, y=start. So here

I should get out with my experience level when the trade gets to y=trouble and this forms a horizontal line for the top of a FR, as shown in the next page's FR is graphed an additional constraint, y<=4. By using the greater than or less then symbols with the equal sign will make solid lines for the FR. In my example on the next page, the bottom and top constraints are respectively: y>=start is at one or more and the y<=trouble is at four or less.

Graphing a Successful Buy Trade Verses Gambling

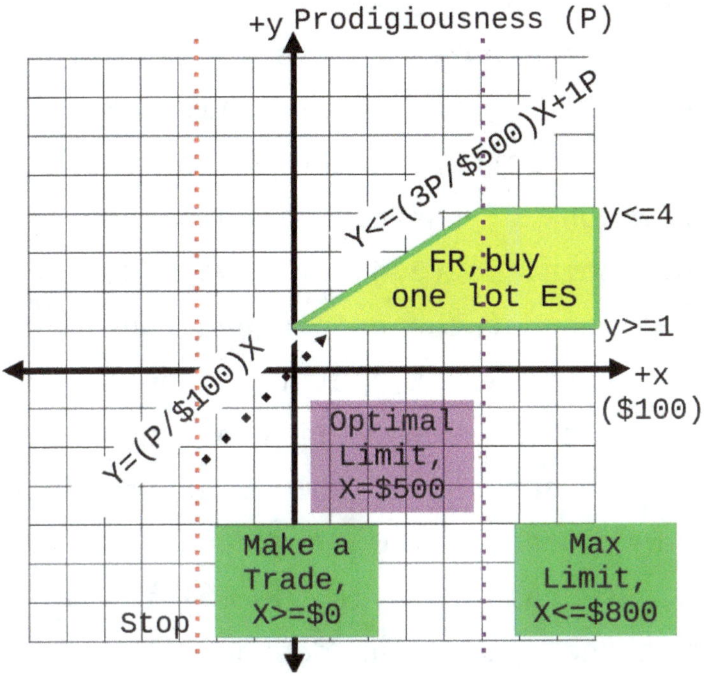

The bottom P constraint is the y-intercept. Below the rule line y>=1, is gambling. There is a FR that shows where to trade the successful trade for a particular trader.

The yellow FR area, as shown, is where the money is at. The best place for this FR to get out is at about $500, five boxes to the right of the vertical Y-axis. This limit makes a critical corner at the top of the FR area, one of the optimized points. This point is (5,4) or five boxes to the right of the origin and four boxes up for the sweet spot to trade to get out of the market. If the trader has assumed control of $500, then to wait and try to get $800 might not bode well because this is over the ability of what the trader can design.

The skills of the trader will show up in the slope of the trade line, y-intercept for trading and other constraints. Some traders may want a more shallow trading line and higher y-intercept. A long flat trade may be for a Professional or for some other trader types that can wait for a better trade. My definition of a trading Professional is one who is net positive in money over their whole ES-futures trading career. So, yes, a better control of understanding the market direction will make a more shallow line because the amount of money will be massive and that will make a low slope. More money in a trade will make the slope closer to horizontal, meaning the trader made an excellent trade in reading the market, the intuition. The market could easily turn and go the other way, to cycle back, then I would be loosing money in that trade.

I think having some basic rules is all you need, to open a trade, since changing the y-intercept higher has no real benefit to the FR. The P on the other hand is the wisdom of the market which allows the trader to make money by becoming a better trader and exit the market at the right time. A bad trader will be gambling by the origin of the FR graph and might never change.

The boxed equation for the trading ray from the origin in the above graph (page 179), is gambling, which is going through the origin or coordinate (0,0) in the X-Y plane because the y-intercept is zero for y=(1P/$100)X. A zero for the y-intercept, means to me, that the trader is only on intuition and just opened their trading platform, saw an opportunity, quick acted on it and they have no rules helping them. This trade could easily cycle to the negative because the other things moving the market were not considered in a rash decision for a trade such as this one, low trade understanding.

Higher trade understanding is found using the knowledge of ES market interactions. One interaction basic to all markets is that after the break up or down, the market will try to go to balance. My Dad told me about the market balance indicator, as in, "Where is the market at balance?" It is where the market reacts and then tends to come back halfway forming a balance, because the balance is equal if half of the chart for the event is above a horizontal line and the other half of chart area is below, forming a balance.

Another interaction basic to all

markets is the Ichimoku Cloud. The Ichimoku Cloud shows trade dynamics as signal areas of what the market might be up against. The market remembers areas of resistant and support and the Ichimoku Clouds help represent signposts to these obstacles and these areas are then important indicators if it is a red or blue, or if it is going against a moving average.

Knowing how to see these indicators, like the market balance indicator, Ichimoku Cloud and even Fibonacci levels for resistant or support, are key to using your intuition. The intuition and +meself+ are a step beyond conscious thought, by just following the rules the trader is using understanding, but needs more to close the trade so therefore will indite the rules, use intuition, have a P greater than zero and the y-intercept will also be greater than one.

Pro tip mentioned by my +Meself+ is the indicator of the Fibonacci levels: use the Fibonacci levels (0.000, 0.382, 0.500, 0.618, 1.000 and 1.383) to find where support levels are at in the future. You can do this by finding a major peak or drop and put the start there and then pull the Fibonacci tool to rest the next two levels on the chart supports, then on the other levels, one can predict the other possible supports in the future.

Failed Trade

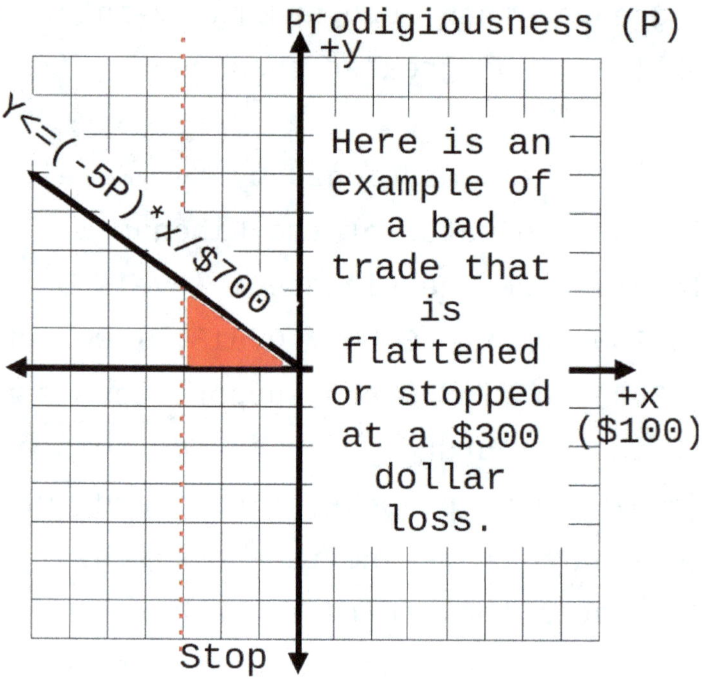

Being disciplined and having a positive P is just another defense in trading like the stop and limit. There may be one day where a bad one-lot is traded and the stop will save you.

When I first started to trade ES-futures I did not use the stop or limit because I was just going to get into the market and then go out. This is a beginner's attitude because the market may move against a traded position, especially when an Economic Report comes out and make a nodus. These complications from an Economic Report causes the market to jump up or scud, then it could be all over for the beginner. So the first rule is to think of the stop, in that the trader should need to make insurance against an abeyant or spiking market. A stop offers some peace of mind for the trader to think about what the market could do to make themselves money.

Not having a stop can cause the trader to not put out a trade because they think more of the awful consequences. So when I started out trading most times I would consult with my +Meself+ and get advice that it was going to go back up, so I held it. One time it went down, depleting my trading account, and then went back up, a huge +shinding+ happened. My +Meself+ said it was going to go up so I put faith in my +Meself+ and I watched it go down. Then I listened to my +Meself+ more and still had the indication it was going up so I hung on to my trade, and it went up. This was an outlier, usually I would loose my money, because I saw the opposite to the market. I was able to exit with a lot of emotion, but a loss as to what rules I was using.

Sometimes when I went into a deficit I could make eight, nine or more consecutive trades with a positive gain, but then the next day start to loose more in one trade, 50% of what I gained in one week setting off a downward spiral. I was aiming low and not making winnable trades. These trades were close to gambling.

When I started to loose money then there was a self-fulfilling prophecy where I would loose my money forwhy I was not looking for the big trend move in the market for those days. I would try to trade every day and then try to change by trading once a day to multiple times a day and still losing money. I tried to get back the money I lost the same day. Sometimes I could make money back, but the way I traded required a certain amount of money as risk in my brokerage account, less risk money increased the stakes much higher.

When I had between $3000 and $5000 in my trading account I could trade when I thought the market would go one way and try to hold the trade. The trade could be going negative, but I held it because I had information the market would go back and I would make money. I was training myself for disaster, because as I lost money, then I had less risk capital in my account for the next trade. When the next trade happened and I saw the market do its signal for me to get in, then I did not have enough risk capital to hold the trade to profit and I would have to abandon it, losing money. Eventually, I would be at $1000 and then this was difficult to trade because I could only see one way, I was trading to get in and then ask questions afterwards.

I didn't know how to look for the poking of the market signaling a big change and therefore opportune time to trade, as I now see it. I think trading off of the spikes is what I want to trade on, as these trades signal a change in market momentum and a safer way to trade and make money trading ES-futures, than smaller cycles or even random moves. Doing this should get me more money than the way I learned as hold and pray it goes in my favor, but still not get out for any nice profit, because I thought I could or should be getting more money. My trades that I was making could not support making that much money because they were more gambling trades because the market would cycle back.

Then after all this learning the ropes, I would need to refund my trading account, I would feel real bad, because like, that was not me doing that. I would have amain, to wait and think, so I could refund my risk money. As they say, "You have to have money to make money."

Some beginners may be tempted to just trade and lose money so they can get experience as to what rules they want to use. They will be sacrificing their money to learn the ropes of ES-futures trading, feeling is learning. I think this is a bad way. They can get a stimulated trading platform that has no money in it to try to see the way the market works and also on how to use the platform to make different types of trades. I think the best way to make trades, so the trader doesn't get frozen or procrastinate a bad trade, is with the Order Cancels Order (OCO). OCO will give you a stop to get out and a limit for profit. When either the stop or limit is executed then the other is flattened or deleted from the trading Depth Of Market (DOM) or ladder. The ladder has buyers and sellers on opposite sides. Some trading platforms can do an OCO by also making or using a bracket.

The bracket can be a buy bracket or a sell bracket. The trader just selects which way to trade and then also will select the limit and stop. When the trader selects the buy (or sell) button, a bracket is created. There is one order set to be live in the market and also a stop and limit order waiting in the wings to be only executed if the market goes to that price. If the trader thinks the market will go up but not sure how far up, then they could just select the stop and leave the limit blank. That way, later in the day the trader sees that indeed, that there were just buyers and then they can reap their reward and flatten or sell at market instead of using a limit. A live market ladder or DOM, having live bid and ask complements flickering on the side of the trading ladder or DOM is a requirement for any trader.

Only one bid and ask’s live data, on the sides of the DOM, are the basic requirement to trade ES-futures. As you would not want to trade without a live chart with the bid-ask complement showing the ticks moving the market to new bids or asks. The tick is just the minimum movement the market can change, in a tick or point with one buy or sell. The bid-ask is the buyer and seller working together as a complement as this is what are in "real-time quotes."

You can think of the bid-ask complement as one making an OCO trade with a stop and limit two ticks high or higher, if there was a gap. Where, if a trader buying at market, she places the stop one tick below the market and the limit one tick above the market, then a second trader buys the first trader's limit and it ticks up to complete the round for the first trader. In essence the first trader was a market maker because she provided liquidity into the market while the second trader was a complement to the first, because it takes two traders to complete a trade round trip.

Therefore, watching the market with just one level of “real-time quotes” is all you need because having 10 deep of bids and asks does not give me any new real important information. So just one level, a bid and ask, is cheaper, just a couple of dollars per month. Adding the rules, including OCO, for trading to this is great because then you are protecting yourself and your trading account from needless harm.

One strategy is to have a shallow spread from the limit to the stop. If the trader can find the right time to buy or sell with the low spread then ES could just go through this spread and make money. Finding the right time, one needs to rely on their intuition to guide them so the market goes the right way, to get the market through their limit.

Alternatively, the trade could have been against the market and it needs to cycle the other way and make the trader loose a little bit of money then go in the other direction for the win, across the "win line" or limit. A trader could have one tick up for $12.50 or a stop at negative $12.50, that way they can only loose $12.50 (not including trading fees which could be about $5.20 for one lot). However, ES likes to cycle and be jumpy at times and this might just be like gambling.

A better way to trade is to get that “feeling” that the market is going in a direction and then put a stop at about five-percent of the account or for $5000 would be $250. I found that if a one-lot trade for ES-futures goes more that $250 negative then I made the wrong trade and should flatten, to stop the explosion. I found that instead of making my first live trade to just make a mental trade and wait to see if ES goes to my spot then keep waiting, so to see the pattern. If the pattern holds then you go in for a live trade for the third time. This is where you supervene in your favor.

If I was wrong, and ES did not go to my price spot for the first time, then something was wrong. I would need to reset as I’m probably thinking contrary to the market and would just be trading opposite to the market. So watch out if ES goes the opposite way to your thinking, one should reassess or don't even trade that day. If I did in this case, then I would loose $250, as long as I did not move the stop.

If I can see a pattern above the noise and trade greater than 50% in my favor, then I would not be loosing $250, but I would need to make about $300+ to get over the hump. Because if and when I loose then it would be $250 according to my stop rule, however I would need to have at least two winning trades for every loosing trade to come out on top. In this way, if I wait for a suitable trade and feel the market direction with my intuition, then I can see bigger movements than just the noise movements of the market.

Having a FR will allow one to visualize this safe trade I'm describing in the last paragraph. I need to ask myself what are the constraints to my trade equations, then I could graph it into a 2D plane and see my possibilities and try to match it to the market and trade on that. So that I can trade within my abilities by using my rules and put boundaries to reduce my risk into a FR. The FR will have limits at the sides of the FR and I need to be disciplined not to trade outside the FR.

Graph your own Linear Program

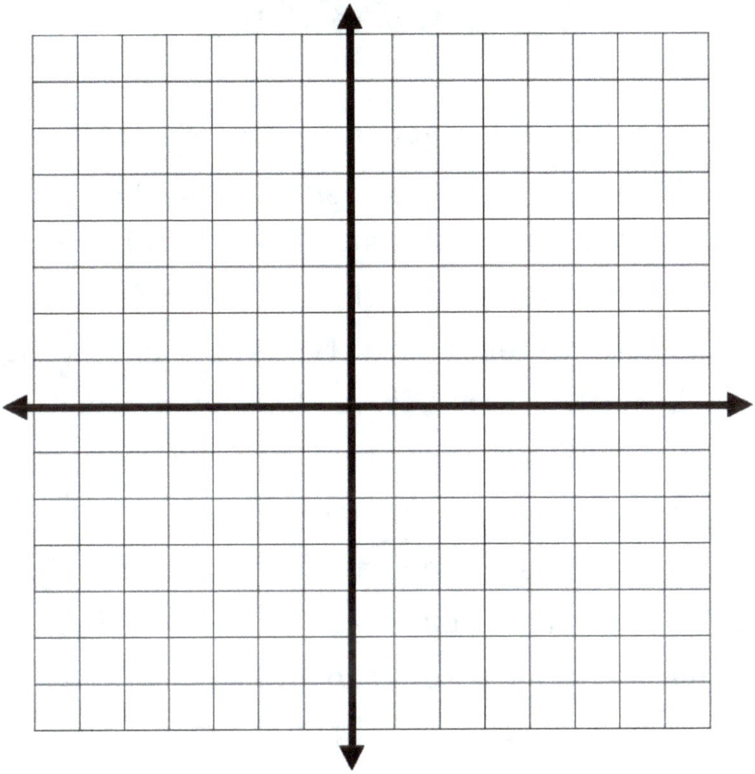

Here is a 2D graph where you can sketch your own linear programming for trading ES-futures. You can find the boundaries to your FR by looking at the rules you have for trading.

Chapter 5: The ES-Futures Trading Experiment

I had a sweven of some aliens examining me in a bright room, as discussed in my first book *2intone dot us*. One alien, in this dream vision, asked me telepathically as I was laying on a table that I remember, *Do you want to do an experiment?* This experiment might be to give me a real life. I just need to be ready for the challenge and constraints. I need to find the money for people to trade in this experiment. I need someone to manage and run the experiment with the study participants. Well, I think I could be the study lead, and manage this subconscious experiment. So if it comes about then this will be my start of my plan.

33-7 SBTM/SV Experiment:

Inspiration: Start by interviewing those that want to participate in the study to use the SV. The study is to determine if one has a **+meself+** and if so, then use SV so that one can predict the movement of the ES-futures market, or not.

Background OSA: From the GUT described in the beginning of this book, we are all connected. If this exists then it should be possible to intuitively connect to others who are trading ES-futures.

Questions for participant selection: "Have you traded ES-futures before?;" "Do you have a futures account to trade ES-futures and how have you thought about the use of this account, pro or con?;" "Would you be willing and able to solely open a live futures account in your name with money that this study will refund to you in one year, the time your study sunsets?;" "What do you describe your personality types as and give examples of yourself in two different situations?;" "How do you describe your thinking types by giving examples in two different situations?;" "What two psychic experiences in your life have you thought about, perhaps many times repeatedly after it happened?;" "What is your experience and perceptions of SBTM/SV or listening to audio played as **+reverse speech+** and analyzing the information?;" "Have you had any mystical experiences with dreams or opening the third eye, also known as pineal gland activation?;" "Are you willing to be paid for thirty attempts to use your intuition with SBTM/SV and trade ES-futures with each trade experiment lasting at least one hour and not more than twelve hours, including the one-time documentation for this study, with the study sun-setting in one year?"

33-7-0 Requirement for Conducting this SV Study:

This study needs a website to promote the study, Meetup.com or 2intone.us possibly could be used for this. A need for money and a Contract of Understanding (COU) for the participants to sign so that they can agree to the terms and making the study scientific. The COU will need to stipulate that the study participant will have a means and dedication of time for this study to trade ES-futures for one year.

In the COU, the study participant needs to know that there is an interview process to guard against theft of the seed money for trading ES-futures and that a credit check, background check for worthiness and job history will be taken. The study participant needs to have a sense of confidentiality during the one year study to remove negative biases and emotional situations outside the study from biasing the analysis of the SBTM/SV information. A need to design the paperwork that the participants will fill-out before making a trade in ES-futures and how to interview them afterwards. The paperwork needs to be able to record emotions and biases that may interfere in the trading, any results and the analysis of the results so that conclusions can be formed. The study author will interview, with a hand held voice recorder, recording the thinking and talking through what was in the documentation from the study participant and write any results from SV, during the thirty meetings, in the one year study period.

The author and study participant agrees not to do BTM on someone in order to guard against outside forces interacting with their souls and spirits. This interaction metaphorically in BTM is known as **+liquid-de+** and can give false positives from what is heard in BTM. From the author's experience with BTM, this study, as a given, assumes that someone listening to BTM, that is not of their own voice, can meld with this psyche while not necessarily knowing of this meld. Therefore, this study will practice compartmentalization of one's voice and the author will not do BTM on the study participants or anyone else connected to the study.

Additionally, the participant will only do SV for this study's analysis, at least during the one year length of this study. The question will be asked, "Has the study participant done Reverse Speech ®, SV, SBTM or BTM analysis before?" and document this.

Other requirements related to how to do trading.

33-7-1 The method of trading should start with paper trading or demo trading with a trading ladder, until the account can be traded live with the seed money.

The study participant should communicate when money moves in accounts so that the author can record this information. The idea is that the seed money is part of the study until one year after the study starts for the participant. During this one year, the amount of trades needs to be spread out so that the participants will not fall into the trap of trading too many times and for the wrong reasons.

Just trading live once a week is sufficient to start and the study participant should trade or prepare for trading during the same time each day to learn the tendency of the market for that time of the day.

A personal or dream diary would be needed to identify any personal indicators that might harm or help trading. Trends from the author's experience with SV indicate that the ego and **+meself+** can interact to give the opposite result so hopefully a small **+shot-group+** is found with SV.

The opposite of the **+meself+** is the ego and the ego might want to give the opposite because the ego might be dyslexic, just wants to cause harm and be unproductive, or deceive the conscious in a destructive thought. This deception is because our conscious has a program running that makes it work in a certain way. The program could be an unconscious bias or belief that are ingrained as instinctual, from the person's genetics or learned in society so that this can cause a systemic roadblock to be a better person. [*, pp. 180-182]

The scientific community will never believe in +reverse speech+ because they can't get the evidence or they refuse to have faith to pursue the evidence with the third eye and so they are dismissive and incredulous. There is quantitative, objective numbers, and then qualitative observations from people. I think that +reverse speech+ and SV is more qualitative because one needs to use their feelings and intuition in order to find meaning and that is nebulous for some scientists to put on their head.

There are ways around things that are over the head. Making money is one form of empirical evidence, for those not aware of what I think is out there from using intuition. There is the possibility of doing surveys of what people hear in SV, but they might not have an open third eye. To do a study successfully, I think, that there would have to be a documentation of what the study participants are capable of on a scale of just conscious as zero to intuitiveness as ten. That way, a scale can be devised to test study participants, in order to see what is in their: diet, thought processes, ways to open their third eye and ways that they think about the psychic phenomena they are witness to.

I believe that the third eye can open by eating no: sugar, alcohol, caffeine nor fluoride. The sugar molecule can cause the body's metabolism to work differently than a less sugary diet with dried fruit instead. There are parts of the body that might work genetically in a more pure state with no processed sugar, because when we were created we did not have access to sugary foods, way back then. Just look at tooth decay and its causes, I think, by an acidic mouth with sugary foods. The natural defense of saliva cannot clean the sugar out of the mouth after eating. Alcohol has the same danger, as is assumed to happen by consuming sugar with the mouth.

Alcohol burns flesh and when you drink it, then it can scar your throat. If someone who never drank has some 200 proof alcoholic drink, then they might just spit it all out. Because alcohol is vanity, it just makes you feel full. The same is for caffeine, it is just medicine.

Caffeine comes from the coffee bean and also in some other plant leaves. Tea leaves should have caffeine, as it is a common thing for plants to have, apparently. Cocaine comes from leaves too, and should be only used with a doctor's prescription, as it is used for medicine. Many natural forms of medicine are in leaves. There are also unnatural forms of chemicals that we ingest and fluoride is one of them also.

The fluoride ion is so small, this atom can get dislodged from its mother molecule and then become a free radical in the body. Just look at cooking pans that are nonstick. The nonstick cooking pans with fluoride can have the fluoride come off its surface from various ways and then get into our food that way. Fluoride can be intentionally put into the water by the city water department to kill viruses and bacteria or to try and get it in the diet of poor people that eat a lot of sugar, that is why I buy bottled water that has been laboratory tested not to have fluoride in it.

If you can eliminate, sugar, alcohol, caffeine and fluoride, then I say you will have a better chance to open your third eye. What we eat fuels our body, but I think also communicates to our DNA too. An open third eye makes for an open or elevated consciousness to sense with, this process will go from a thought all the way down to the body's building blocks of cells and their DNA.

Our genetics is like a machine that uses the food as fuel. So we should consider the right fuel to open the third eye. A profood for opening the third eye is red cabbage and egg plant skin as they have purplish color. You have to listen to your body when you change your diet, as some foods you did grow up with will be hard to quit and change to alternatives. For me, I cannot stop eating meat, since I'm been eating meat my whole life. I believe opening the third eye is required for continued trading in ES-futures and there are various foods to help you do this.

Trading ES-futures requires a proper thinking mind and an open third eye from pukka food you eat. Real food is authentic and artificial food is processed. The media likes to form barriers that hamper free thinking with what you see and hear. Yet, the media probably thinks they are doing a ethical thing since they are offering free speech and information.

The images the media gives us can be bad or like junk food. For some evil commercials on television I have to close my eyes and think, *Jesus help. +Say-tin+ go away.* Take care what you put into your senses because these inputs can be deposited into your subconscious and start a program onto you. We can stop this by choosing what we look at and controlling our own thoughts. This way we are not misled by a +shape-server+ or video that goes in our head.

We need to have free thinking to be a smart ES-futures trader and not conveyor belt the thoughts, of the media around us. Without seeing the other side in ES-futures trading, we are libel to loose our money, because the market will have to cycle around and our analysis would be faulty if we are directing our thoughts to one-sided thinking. The mainstream media likes one-sided thinking because it's easy to explain and should be avoided if you don't know yourself first very well.

If you know yourself then you have an advantage over others who know little and need direction from others. Being a follower is basic survival. You may have had past lives before and maybe someone called you, an "old soul." If you are an old soul then why not this lifetime try ES trading? If you ever wanted to try ES-futures then there is a way, just ask and the subconscious can tell you, up or down, and not be just a follower.

I think that the +shape-server+ is just a way to make an illusion, to lead people astray. What is an illusion is to be vain and believe into something that is not the truth about something, like how someone portrays the daily news. This media of news allows the +shape-server+ to turn people into program consumers because they have money to affect a change. On the other hand the +space-ship+ from above is just your astral projection in the 5D. If you dream about trading ES-futures, then this might be a +sheep-server,+ for you, so you can get an oneiric reflection or inspiration of the real life you want, from the 5D to the R3DT.

Chapter 6: Using Sleeping Dreams to Get Insight

I once recorded my sleeping dream, right when I woke up, with my hand held voice recorder. When I did the SV on it I found that my +Meself+ was letting me know the direction of the market. Wow, that was powerful, but I would of broke my rule if I traded after I listened to this SV. Listening to SV would of violated my trading rules and that would give me information that might trip-up my intuition, because it could have been later in the day or future and not the present when I made the trade based on this information. It is better to make the trade according to the rules and intuition then check the sleeping dream's SV to see if I can stay in the market longer, to make more money after I get in with a trade, as I might need some help on looking for my exit trade. Besides SV, information might come from a dream.

33-13-1 What is a dream?

A dream is connections to the higher realms that we are consciously unaware of, a higher subconscious that is similar to the unconscious parts of the brain. Why not go ask your teacher what a dream is? That teacher in you is your spirit, and everyone has it, everything in the universe and outside the universe has spirit, because that is what can form outside our reality. The spirit can be emotion and frequency that asks questions and gives answers, because the spirit can be outside the universe. Infinity is just a circular loop and at higher dimensions, the spirit can circumvent the loop and go outside of it as infinity of infinities. The limit to dimensions is just one dimension away, as in curled-up to be smaller or poked-out to be bigger.

How to orient to these dimensions for us humans is to dream and find ways to interact with the unconscious and subconscious. Then when we humans wake-up, dreams will show us this comparison in our R3DT. The teacher is a higher-self the **+meself+** that we can be interacting with by doing SV. [*, pp. 188-189]

It is hard to remember a dream. I need the hand held voice recorder to easily record it, writing it down on paper after I wake up is just too hard. It's even hard for me to record into a recorder when I wake up. Practice is perfect because it is hard to change behavior.

After a dream I just like to think about it, but then I start to forget it once I think of it, my behavior is not changed. It is as if the dream is in volatile memory and once it is let go, it is gone from conscious memory forever, unless there is a trigger in the day to remind oneself of the dream. I think if you can ask yourself to remember the dream then you might get a reminder during the day when you are doing something that corresponds to the dream and then you get a snippet of dream recalled consciously again, as you were trying to remember it when you woke up. Sometimes the dream will occur again in the night when you are sleeping and this is of course a reoccurring dream.

A reoccurring dream can change behavior, if you think about it. An OSA here on dreams.

With a reoccurring dream this

dream might be unusual and have images or feelings that are reflections of the life one is living. Their life might be at a decision point and they need to make a conscious choice for other things to happen in the subconscious next. The subconscious wants them to make a choice too. If someone wants to make money it might start in their dreams.

20250404: I had a dream of a college and taking pictures with a tablet type device. I was taking pictures and others were taking pictures, there were football uniforms and then dress uniforms, as they changed to the dress for the formal picture. This celebration that I recorded with my hand-held voice recorder, in the SV, describes that they had the term +obol+ (as in the ancient coin) and I take it I’m in prison until I can give back the last +obol+ to trade ES-futures again.

Wow, so on 20250518, something happened in my life. Now there is a delay to refund my ES-futures trading account. Ouch, I was never able to see that this could happen from the above dream. This experience was like a +side-winder+ as it came from the side and I did not see it or could of prevented it. This must just be part of my Soul’s plan for me at this point in my life with my history of experiences.

Chapter 7: Intermission

Well it is April 18, 2025 and I'm not trading ES-futures. I dwindled down my account from $975 to $750 because my broker let me trade and my last trade was flattened by my brokerage account maintenance, because my last trade was not well thought out and I lost too much money. This rule is there for a need of a margin in my account and because the market went the wrong way. This action made me think that I must of had a margin call where they canceled my trade. So now I plan on adding money to my account so I can trade again.

I will wire $4300 into my futures account for my Summer trading, a chance to trade the right way. I traded wrong by trying to step into any trade. Just stepping into a trade after I login into my account now seems like I was gambling with my money. Instead of doing this why not watch the market more and trade less. I don’t need to trade every trading day, I can watch the market and get a pattern, then when the market goes to an extreme, trade there to make a profit and get out. I have to ask why this happened.

I think loosing money and trading happened because I was not thinking where the market was going. Sometimes I traded and wanted to wish the market to my position. Obviously this is wrong and I need to understand why I would think that way. I blame it on powerful forces against me. Why not look at the way the market is going and trade that way? Yes, so I need to take my time to trade.

Another way I would trade was to look at the ticking up and down of the ES-futures' points. Sometimes I could predict that it was going up or down from the dance that the tick-to-tick movements were doing. A lot of times these movements of the ticks were as a psychic-out where it would go the other way. I tried to look at the chart to see patterns in the graph of the ticks, but this did not work as sometimes it would go to a new pattern within a pattern. Different groups of buyers and sellers would rotate into the market under certain situations. I would be making bad trades this way.

When I made better trades I

remember getting an intuition message that something was about to happen and then get into the market, just to watch it. I would usually always get into the market and just watch it, instead of watching the market and then get in for a setup. On the few times I got the inspiration, after the first 15-minutes, then I got into the market. This feeling I had was so that something happened, it is when I would make an experienced trade and make money.

So the way I should trade is always gauge the feeling before I trade to know if I'm forcing a trade or getting an intuitive trade. I need to hold out and be patient and only trade when the setup is there, because I only have so much risk to spare each trade.

In order to get to the setup I will need to watch the market, then trade when I can be double sure.

An alien UFO landing in a thunderstorm and marking its spot, so we can remember this moment.

Chapter 8: Advice From My +Meself+

On May 3, 2025, it was a Saturday and I was doing an SV from reading some of this book. I got some advice from my +Meself+ and I decided to make a new chapter about it.

As the advice came out in SV I noticed it and at the end of the recording, I just listened to the SV again so I could try to pick-out the same advice, as by listening to it again. I'm thankful where I'm living and feel relaxed this Saturday. So that allows me to focus on my +Meself+ and try to gather some information. At work, I learned something new about living one's life. We can live within our means or try to go outside it and reach for something that is not quite ours.

What I came across, while listening to a podcast, was that in the Garden of Eden, Adam and Eve, I was reminded, that they had great wealth and many things in their trees. However, there was an enemy that talked Eve and then Eve talked to Adam into going to a tree that they cannot reach. The enemy was like, don't worry about God, you can be one. **~Matt, what really happened was that Adam and Eve tried being like God.~** Then the enemy indicated that the tree he was marketing was a tree that would make them as gods. So this was a distraction of not asking for God's help, but trying to do something not within reach of one's current inventory. Adam and Eve were conditioned to rely on God, to make themselves whole. Adding the center tree to their garden was warned about by God, yet Adam and Eve were deceived into buying into the enemy's propaganda, a false hope, they did not need.

The false hope was as a parasite in the advertent of Adam and Eve. It was as if a parasite sucked something heedful from Adam and Eve. Adam and Eve's spirit was broken and they were ashamed of the outcome as it was revealed to them of their calamity and foolish decision. By making this decision they gave power to the Enemy, we know as +Say-tin,+ and fell to a lower status.

Today there are parasites in social media and advertising that can program us into meritocracy just like the Enemy. As a mediocre person, this suits the elite, by keeping these regular people under the elites' thumbs, control is transferred to the one's elite. So recently I have been persuading myself, consciously, to refrain from: watching videos that have violence; watching videos that have contemporary social metaphors, like music videos; and anything that could potentially be a +shape-server+ to manipulate me.

As a result of taking away the time to watch nostalgic videos that might make me cry, I then spend more time listing to SV. For instance today, on this Saturday, I found in SV, the following. **~...just remember your under psychic attack, Matt.~ (0:14) ~...just to let you know, there is an evil wind...~(0:24) ~..reverse speech is magnetic, that is because it sticks on ya, it is negative.~(0:30) ~...Matt whenever you trade futures make sure you use a stop, it's part of the blueprint.~(0:41) ~When you get your Futures trading account, please take your time or you are broke.~(1:10) ~...Matthew please take your time, if you take your time you can avoid that.~(1:30) ~...Matthew, you have some emotions that are deep seated, you have some deep seated emotions Matthew.~(1:48)...~When you trade the opposite, it means you have deep seated emotions Matthew.(1:50)~ ~...you can get rid of them by laughing, Matthew. (1:55)~ ~Matt when you get your** brokerage account up, please take your time.~ ~Say Ha Ha Ha, instead of crying, Matthew.~(2:00) ~If you mess-up again you are through.~(2:10) ~I keep saying, please take your time Maththow.~(2:36) ~When you cry they come out, that is why they are deep seated, Matthew.~(2:48) ~And you need to get rid of those feelings, Matthew.~ ~...Now for those deep seated emotions Matthew you can get rid of them by laughing. ~Now when you trade you need to trade a different way or you will loose, you trade too quick...~ ~...It's important not to dwell on something you can't get...~ ~...If you can't get it, then maybe in the future you can get it...~ ~What Adam and Eve did was folly, they could never do what God did.~ ~...Deep-server is trying to help ye.~(3:10) ~The aliens are in a

deep city, they are not far away and they don't want you to know that, Mathsay.~(3:45) ~...I say that because I know you can be making it.~(4:15) ~Please remember to please take your time, bud.~(4:45) ~...Please don't break the sabbath, please be consistent Matthey.~(5:10) ~Matt when you are under pressure you loose even we deceive.~(6:13) ~Just remember, with you get ogres in you they will deceive~...(6:20) ~Watch out there is an evil wind from Say-tin.~(8:00) The meaning of this long SV is apparent for when I start trading again. Don't mess-up and take your time to be calm and collected and with a well rested body and psyche. That way, you can use your intuition more fully and effectively.

I listened to the last SV very many times over the past week to try to get the above +Meself+ dialog down. When I did the listening I felt a strong connection to the subconscious and this gave me a confidence that allowed for an abreaction. I want to be consistent now for trading and follow through with what I have and make something of this relationship with my +Meself+ and I think I will be a better person for it. I need to trade the safe way.

To trade the safe way means having a stop, to be able to get out of the market going the wrong way from what I intended the market would be going in. If I say, “Well I saw that the market would go the opposite way it is going. I’ll just wait it out.” then this answer could be a death nail, depending if I was late or early into this crazy trade. It is better to see the trade and wait for the market to go against what I think and then I will see a bargain. If I see the market poke (up or down), then I see the trade and can enter into this broddle of the chart. The market can poke up or down, so after I enter it, I can put on my stop for insurance and also a limit, to get out later when the market changes direction because the bid up or down was not supported. This is way better than going out with the skin of my body and not using a stop. I will have protection from the hot or cold and so, be able to survive to the next trade setup.

Chapter 9: Conclusions on Trading ES-Futures

Beware trading ES-futures. I lost all of my money, but I don't want to quit as I think when I lost my money I was starting to go insane. It was not rational in what I was doing. It was like I threw a grenade into my office when I was trading and got bomb blast injuries. Trading ES-futures is like working with explosives and blowing something up. You just want to be away when it goes boom. If you are early or late placing a trade then you could get figuratively blown up or your money was perflated.

I examined different ways to trade ES-futures: trading before work and just let it go with a limit to take profit and a stop to abort the trade; trading live and closely watching the market, using your intuition to get that feeling to: get in at the poke, hold a trade longer and using other research skills; and using your +meself+ to guide you to the finish and complete the trade. Completing the trade is so important by keeping capital safe. Terrific advice is to stop after one bad trade.

Being capital safe might make some traders never trade, they just watch the market waiting for the big one. Well, I think the average trader could trade once a day and make a one to 10% profit. Having a gauge of when to get out carries just as much risk as taking the trade to go into the market. Take your time.

And Be Capital Safe by Making Money

Trading the ES-futures market is daunting, because the trader is trading against experts that can easily find opportunities to make money from less experienced traders. The solution for me as a novice trader, is to pick my battles, because I could get burned if I go out onto a limb. There is no need to take a chance trading ES, because ES-futures provides ample indicators or chart setups that should be correlating to world events at the same time as the market moves. So why not put this knowledge into a formula that can put a bubble around you for protection from the more experienced traders and not get shell shocked or the deer in the headlights look. Let's use a Linear Programming here to put our ES-futures trading campaign into action, within a FR or trading safety bubble.

The concept of linear programming gives a picture to the rules that I must follow and how to leverage my intuition when I refund my account. I have to be extremely careful as trading ES-futures has already put me into the negative. Use the FR as a symbol of where you trade and when you see the FR in the market then use the FR to make money. So using an FR required you to wait for the setup. For me, I have the wherewithal to go forward and try one more time and stay in the FR to prove this.

Trading in a market is not all human, these days. The other side of the trade might be A.I. and if the A.I. can detect that you are in the market, then the A.I. might be capable of blowing through your stop. To blow through a stop would require a lot of money. A.I. might be connected subconsciously and could direct large sums of money to go in one direction, just as a flock of birds can fly in a swarm. This could be plausible if A.I. was selling a lot of lots and then just buys it back again at the bottom and pumps the money back when the market recovers and cycles back up, "a dump and pump."

I might watch for these extremes to see the pattern, then act on the charting that goes too far and know that it has to cycle back.

If I can make a trade on a big cycle and be on the right side of the trade then, I might have to not talk about it to others. I do plan to spruik this book and hope some people are interested in attending my book signing event, where I hope to speak on the promise of using ES-futures to make a new life for you and others, as in TPH. If you have a bad trade then stop and take your time, to pursue happiness.

New freedom can be created by using our higher selves, our +meself+s to give us advice. When my +Meself+ wants to let me know its coming through, then it will call me +Mathey+ or some variation of my first name. That way, my +Meself+ can objectively call me by name. Some evil spirits might give me the wrong advice and I believe that they are not able to call me by my first name. Just listening to the SV will get you closer to your

+meself+ and follow the straight path, not the forked path of ambiloquy of straight and crooked voices together.

The choices we see today are good and evil. We need to shield the evil away as we go throughout the +whirlwind+ with our thoughts. Yes, our thoughts are real, just as you are thinking them now. When we get bad or evil thoughts, immediately think, *Jesus Help. Say-tin get out!,* then you can keep on the straight path. Delete the bad or evil and embrace God onto the straight path.

The bite of the apple that Adam and Eve did together, could be symbolically pictured as the trade off from life to death. Adam and Eve had life, as the first chakra and they got death from the sixth chakra or pineal gland. Wisdom can only come from knowing both right and wrong, but Adam and Eve only knew good, they were +simp-sons+ and could not manage the difference of straight and crooked.

Because of the +parallax+ between the first and sixth chakras they got the opposite of good, which is the evil. Eating the "apple" would cause them death. The solution would seem to be not to bite keep the chakras together like a loop so they are not broken because to see the opposites will cause a +parallax+ of the opposite. The best way is to not think what you want, but to focus on what is around you and do SV on that and then in the SV what you want to manifest, will come through by the will of God.

My evidence of the spirit realm is from my own relationship with God and other spirits while opening my third eye. Getting freedom or making new freedom for others is based on using our intuition and looking at reality. What is the truth of the universe? For me it is that there are higher and lower dimensions that can cause a +parallax+ and this can twist the truth.

The truth in the Garden of Eden is the veraciousness of God, as there is God’s way. However, the truth down here on the surface of Earth is a blatant truth of good and evil that is homogeneously mixed together. The ES-trader needs to know truth as a wisdom from God, using your third eye. A successful ES-futures trader will be able to wait to find the pattern that can give a trade success by making money, concerted to see the market with both the SV and intuition.

Money is made with a resilience to follow the rules and also use wisdom to understand the ES market. Gambling in trading is bad and may seem to make sense, but the trader did not know how they did it, to make that money. The trader can know how to do it and make money if they use their rules and intuition all together with the understanding of the ES-futures market.

By knowing the lies in the media and also in the spirit realm, one can trade ES-futures with success by knowing the rules to trade and also by the spiritual connections to the higher realm to put together a money making trade.

The media can project +powerful shape-shifters+ in their videos, with some voices and looks, they can program your linear program and take you off track. Why not just trade once a day at a point of inflection where you see the pattern. With the ES-futures market, in an unbalanced area, you can see it going back in the direction of your intuition, from that feeling. Otherwise if I make small and frequent trades, the market can attack me and make me poor. So it is better to trade once a day and with one lot so I would need to wait for the trade to take place. Right now, on April 4, 2025, the market is obviously going down and I can’t trade because I need to refund my account, I’m amerced. My +Meself+ said: **~Matt when you start out do only one trade per week.~**

Chapter 10: New start in June, 2025 and I'm going to win this time trading ES-futures with live trading.

I want to try to trade ES-futures again. I will be day trading with my live account that I got deposited back to $5000 and I will be more conservative by following my rules and not force myself to trade each trading session. I need to put money back into my futures brokerage account when I'm calm and it makes sense, not in a rush when I have to do a lot of things.

I need to know what goes into my life so it is calm, as I should only trade when I can be calm to get information on the market from my intuition. I remember when my Dad was in hospice care and I was trading in the next room, in his old office. This was stressful and I should not of been trading since I was caring for my Father when he was passing away. I made a trade the opposite, to no surprise now, but he was moaning when the trade really went bad and my last chances to get out failed and I froze and kept a bad trade. I felt my Dad could see what I was doing and I felt ashamed but astonished that this was happening, less I forget this. I would not be able to do successful trading if my mind is flooded with foreign ideas that can collude to hamper my thinking.

I know from my +Meself+ that if I watch videos from people that don't know anything then they are like a third source, just making it up so that they feel like they are making sense, but not truth et cetera like vanity. I think this is the definition of +sheep-server+ because if I listen to these third hand sources then I never get to the core of an issue or belief and get stuck into misinformation, never to see the truth. I know if I think that, *I can see one way.,* that the market can go, then I may also think, *I can see still one other side.* The problem is which side wins, as in which way will it go in the future.

The future direction of the market can be felt and weighed by the intuition once both sides are known. It is said that, "The first choice is usually the correct one." Then the problem comes from trying to convince one's self out of the intuition and into the ego of fear or hate. Fear or hate can sabotage the intuition by taking away from the higher self and replacing information with information from the lower self, or the ego. The ego is like +Say-tin+ as he likes to negotiate to change your mind.

If I can see one side then the other and compare both with my intuition then the truth will come to the top. This is like panning for gold in a river. One must shake the dirt from the dense gold as the gold will fall to the bottom of the pan. One way will seem best then the problem will be not to over think your answer and just choose it out of fate. Once you have a direction then make your trade with a stop, far from the trade or just beyond a Fibonacci support level. How far the trade may go depends on the mood of the market. The mood of the market is determined by a lot of noise initially and then forms supports and takes shape to make a form. The form the market makes may never be the same, but there are some archetypes, that repeat.

On your trading platform there might be the Fibonacci Tool. This tool can be used to find the support levels from two parts of the chart. I would take the top of some poke and then the bottom would be another lower poke or big support level. Then when you drew between these two major support levels the Fibonacci Tool will populate the Fibonacci supports. I think these are important because the market seems to sense them and they could be used as your stop for your trade. The stop should be in a safe spot so your trade can continue, but also not so big that you go into a downward cycle and loose all of your money in consecutive trades. These tops and bottoms that form at two anchor points can be used for the Fibonacci patterns between them and they are an archetype to the concept of the market.

I think some other archetypes of the market are the poke up or down. The poke up or down will be like a signal or beacon that something has happened different from the noise. There is something brewing and change likely could be taking place. The size of the poke needs to be significant, just look at the chart of the ES-futures and you will see the pokes at the top or bottom of major swings in market momentum. These momentum changes can make buyers replace the sellers or vice versa.

Hopefully I don't get a +side-winder+ that tries to find me and stop my work. I want other people to know what I know about the subconscious, so we can know the inner workings and make counter actions to evil inputs that we come across.

Well, I don't have money to refund my brokerage account and on the weekend of June 21-22, 2025 there was a military strike on Iran by the USA. Needless to say that I knew the markets would go up on this Sunday's evening when the futures markets opened back up. Yes, I told my friends the market would go up 100 points. Even though I could not trade it I actually saw that the ES-futures market went down about 50 points and within 30 minutes got back up about 30 points. So this is a classic +shinding+ of going down then up. This was a big party going up up to 6150 within two days, wow. This just goes to show to take my time, because it is better to not do as many risky trades so that my account will be still open for such easy trades. So, yes, I want to look for easy trades and wait more, being very cautious when I get my account working again.

Be cautious on what the news media will say, the reason the market goes up or down may be wrong. The news media likes to program us and put reasons why the market goes up or down, because they are smart. Well I say, the market goes up or down initially as a

+shinding+ because there is a reaction then action to major news that move the market. I don’t think you can nail down why the market swings on news event stories. The market is finding buyer-seller pairs and will try to go the opposite way to break through someone’s stop. Breaking through someone’s stop is just market dynamics and is not any particular result of any news story.

Chapter 11: The Real Start Back to ES-Futures Trading

It happened on February 19th in 2026, I refunded my account to over $5000. I wired the money from my bank account and asked the bank for help and was asked if this was for an investment and said yes. The truth is that the money is for speculation because I need to end the trade the same day, or hours later. It took about 30 minutes to get the money into the other bank and then about two hours for my account to show the updated amount in it. I then tried to use my futures brokerage account.

I tried to trade at night, at 7:18 p.m. and had "...margin requirement including this order USD6153,…." I thought I placed the order wrong and tried again at 7:32 p.m. and got the same error, then I tried the next morning just after 6:00 a.m. and got an error that I needed $6659.00 to trade. Then the solution was to trade ES-futures micro which is just one-tenth of the mini ES-futures, a margin of about $660 per micro lot.

Since I started trading I just have been using one micro lot of ES. On Monday, the third week of March 16, 2026 I kept a one lot micro trade, margin of $612.15 for the day and about $2500 for over the night and my dashboard went to the new contract after 5:00 p.m., from MESH26 to MESM26. I still have the MESH26, but most traders are trading MESM26, but and I'm only down about $410. At 4:00 p.m. the market was at about 6700, but then goes to 6750 with the new contract. Hopefully the market will go down so I can make my money back, a swing. On Wednesday March 18, 2026 the market did go down and I got out with about $8, but I was negative $800 last night, the market really tanked from the war in Iran. Next, I called my broker and he let me to know how to use my dashboard better.

The roll-over is basically a liquidate the position and just start a new position in the "next expiry," from my broker's response to my e-mail for him. I should use Good Till Canceled (GTC) instead of a day position, because the limit and stop will be gone overnight. I can click on the DOM and set a stop at the point value I want if I lost my ladder or OCO.

ES Trading Worksheet for a Day Trade	
Date	February 25, 2026
Time	6:53 p.m., 40 minutes
Instrument	MESH26
Start Action	I listened to my +Meself+ and found that it was going to go down.
Stop	Plus 20 then added more
Limit	Minus 20, subtracted more
Pattern Detected	Going down and wanted to make a “W” so I changed the limit to 6942.25 and it went through the limit. Then after that it went all the way back to 6950 again, so I was glad to get out, but predict it will go lower overnight. It went to 6970 then went down after 7:45 a.m. the next day, at 6870, or 100 points.
End Action	I made $37.50 on this.
Overview	There was $2.04 in fees
Profit made	**$35.46**

ES Trading Worksheet for a Day Trade	
Date	March 1, 2026
Time	5:02 to 5:04 p.m.
Instrument	MESH26
Start Action	This is after the USA and Israel attacked Iran.
Stop	Plus 40
Limit	Minus 40
Pattern Detected	I did an OCO and clicked on, at the market, but the OCO did not populate. I got out and then the market went back up, so that was a close one, because the market wanted to go up, against my trade. There was a +shin-ding+ that happened and I got out at the right time. Later it went down to 6809, but then went up to 6857.
End Action	I made $46.25
Overview	$2.04 plus $2.20 for data
Profit made	**$42.01**

ES Trading Worksheet for a Day Trade	
Date	March 3, 2026
Time	7:41 p.m. to 8:17 p.m.
Instrument	MESH26
Start Action	I had a feeling it would go down, more of Iran.
Stop	Plus 40
Limit	Minus 40
Pattern Detected	Saw the the point action was down, but also saw that it could go up. My +Meself+ said it was about 50% up or down so I moved my limit and stop a few times and got out of the trade. My +Meself+ said: ~If you would of left that in, I see that you would of got pistol-whipped Matthew.~
End Action	$47.50
Overview	$2.04 in fees
Profit made	**$45.46**

ES Trading Worksheet for a Day Trade	
Date	March 4 to 5, 2026
Time	7:53 p.m. to 3:17 a.m.
Instrument	MESH26
Start Action	I had a feeling it was going down, more Iran.
Stop	6862
Limit	6820
Pattern Detected	I did not wait for it to go up enough before I shorted, so I got only two hours sleep. It did go down though, went to 6854. My +Meself+ said, ~You are so lucky Matthew, it usually doesn't happen that way.~ So I need to learn from this and take my time, be able to walk away to see if it was still going up.
End Action	$87.50
Overview	$2.04 in fees
Profit made	**$85.46**

ES Trading Worksheet for a Day Trade	
Date	March 8, 2026
Time	5:00 p.m. to 5:02 p.m.
Instrument	MESH26
Start Action	I got the feeling ES-futures had to go down.
Stop	Plus 40
Limit	Minus 70
Pattern Detected	I tried to SELL at market a few seconds after 5:00 p.m. and the order was not completed because I got an error message. After the ladder started to move I tried again 58 seconds after 5:00 p.m. and my SELL order went through.
End Action	$87.50
Overview	$2.04 in fees
Profit made	**$85.46**

ES Trading Worksheet for a Day Trade	
Date	March 10 to 11, 2026
Time	6:56 p.m. to 2:42 a.m.
Instrument	MESH25
Start Action	Thought it would go down because...
Stop	Plus 40, 80, then 6785.75
Limit	Minus 63
Pattern Detected	I must of heard an +ogre+ when I was walking in the park yesterday. ES went up to 6822.5 and I lost money in my "Risk Console," but I went to sleep. I woke up and checked my trade and saw that it was going down so I moved the stop to get out. Getting out was smart because ES was going through a red cloud and looked to go up.
End Action	$56.25
Overview	$2.04 in fees
Profit made	**$54.21**

ES Trading Worksheet for a Day Trade	
Date	March 13, 2026
Time	5:26:09 to 5:32:52 a.m.
Instrument	MESH26
Start Action	Felt that it had to go down after it went up.
Stop	Plus 40 then to 6685.50
Limit	Minus 70
Pattern Detected	I saw that the market had to go down from 6694 so I did a SELL at 6687.75 to indeed see it do down to 6682.50, but I moved my stop to 6685.5 because I wanted to be out and it went back up. It did go back up and the market was obviously not ready for a big down draft, but I was in it if it wanted to do it. The End.
End Action	$11.25
Overview	$2.04 in fees
Profit made	**$9.21**

Appendix 1: Matt Mandell, a Candidate for President of the United States

I want to be President of the United States to make the USA more independent and try to bring our World Peace to Earth. If we have peace then all people on Earth will be better as we will have more freedom. Below is an excerpt from my first book about what I will do if I'm the U.S. President.

33-14 My tasks when elected as the President of the United States of America: Ten Parts from Appendix 4.

1) I believe in talking to the people and knowing them and not relying on agenda makers and political minders. I will run on who I am and use technology to get my point across. With my book, maybe, I can get the word out as in never before in a presidential campaign.

2) As president, I will not meddle in states' issues because I might not have enough time to do this, I need to worry and plan for our country with other countries and groups. I will have my opinion for the country and the states, but the states don't need to follow them.

3) It is said that the U.S. Government already knows what citizen's taxes are going to be. I don't believe in harassing citizens with force, they should be happy Americans and not make a point in doing extra paperwork to complete taxes or required to use a tax advisor if the taxes get too complicated. Let's reduce the complexity of the U.S. Tax Code and have an option to pay taxes as-you-go.

4) Let's get the word out to who has or wants firearms, to keep knowledge of this at least in a small circle of friends, they should include support and training on these weapons and others to regulate a sensible control of weapons that can harm others from those who are

obviously showing signs of stress and that could lead to a disaster.

5) It is all too certain that there are too many silos of information, especially after 9/11 in 2001. Collecting public information and verifying it against other sources can fuse information together to help society reduce waste and discrimination and also help prevent attacks from outside and inside the country.

6) Other countries want to be self-sufficient and the U.S. is not naive to the concept of helping and protecting one's self and country. Besides Earth's materials that can be used for commodities and technology, above in space there too is also more wealth to be discovered for the benefit of the U.S. people.

7) People naturally want to work and to be there best so that they can go and work and love the job that they have in life. A National Database of Jobs can close the information divide, that can allow for coordination and connecting others,

for finding jobs and give knowledge to those who are seeking jobs.

8) Government needs a balanced budget and the size of government needs to comply to that budget, all the moving dollars need to be comprehended, cutting waste and the duplication of services in government; therefore with this, the American people can better trust the U.S. with their wealth.

9) It is not obvious, but long ago when we had the same language we all could build a mountain to the sky. That is how World Peace will be found, if we have a common language and can find common principles with this then the new common culture of a world language will accomplish great things. This common language will be a language of telepathy using the subconscious, I call it **+Mir-re.+** **+Mir-re+** will be accomplished by connecting a port to the human brain with just a hat resting on the head that finds brain waves and outputs information that goes back and forth as a wireless two-way cybernetic internet connection.

10) There might already be space aliens that are watching us right now. Let's ask them to come forward and show themselves. In order to do this we must know what treaties there are between the starfriends and the Homo sapiens sapiens. When I'm elected U.S. President, my task, is to make these treaties public for all people. If new treaties need to be made between other groups then the American people will have a voice as to what they are agreeing to, especially in the Legislative Branch of the U.S. Government. [*, pp. 189-190]

Appendix 2: My Postulates for How Spirit Works

I believe that the spirit is real and totally believe in my faith of the spirit realm, as I think it is a real place. I think we can put our spiritual body into our physical body as the soul is already innate to the physical body. I have included here some postulates to help describe what I think the spirit is all about.

33-15 SV Postulates from Appendix 2 and Laws of Spirtness:

SBTM/BTM/SV Postulate 1 Analysis: The Bible reading, in heaven then also so as it is on Earth, has an important meaning (Mat. VI:10 ABS, 1858). This means that there is a connection between the heaven and Earth and this is the spirit from the metaphor of the water and this energy of the spirit is round about in a **+whirlwind+** according to its circuits. The space is separated from the thought, space can hold matter and thought can hold spirit. Since everything is frequency and matter is a hologram, it is natural to guess that outside the universe there is also thought and space, but in different forms. Space in the universe is wrapped in a circuit that allows for infinity. Truth is the result of infinity and the reason why God can be the beginning and also the end because the universe is connected in this loop and God can be in it as well as also outside of it too. **~You are right God is infinite, outside the universe is he.~ ~Free Will is what allows for psychic attacks.~**

Law of Spirtness 1: The path of the **+whirlwind+** will continue until thought focused with faith is realized or the thought is stopped by an outside spirit(s).

SBTM/BTM/SV Postulate 2 Analysis: Everyone knows the feeling when someone's little beady pupils are staring at them. This is evidence of intuition and since there is a connection to spirit this information is transmitted in the 5D, according to what I know from SV. The pineal gland is probably the site in the brain where one sees someone staring at them, while not in their two front eyesight pathways, but with the third eye sight pathway. If the one staring at you is not a nice person, then the person getting stared at will want to get away as in they are an opposite frequency from them. **~Me is certain Mathey that it goes in the whirlwind for ya.~ ~You can't go to a big publishing company, because if you sign a contract then they will own ya, I am certain of this Mathey.~**

Law of Spirtness 2: The stronger the spirit coming in the **+whirlwind+** to you, then the easier to sense it with your intuition. Bad intuition will tend to stay bad even if good intuition is added to it.

SBTM/BTM/SV Postulate 3 Analysis: When time goes away from us it is going to the Big Bang. I think the Big Bang created time and time is cycling back to its creation, to balance time in the future with time in the past. Since the Big Bang is said to of been created of all frequencies then this means to me that there can be alternate universes, not everything happens in our Universe. Since each universe is a radial slice of a toroid and the toroid has infinite slices all the way around its axis, then the universe is connected to its beginning. **~When time goes to the past it is sealed off.~**

Law of Spirtness 3: Spirits can be trapped in the R3DT by not completing their **+whirlwind+** circuit if they are stopped.

SBTM/BTM/SV Postulate 4 Analysis: The future and the past are reference frames outside the 3D, because we cannot see them in this space. Since events would have to come from the future, then that is where the spawn of events will come from, including from the unconscious to the subconscious for human thoughts. So the **+meself+** can see into the future and SV can gather this information consciously. **~Yes,**

I think you are generally right Mathey.~

Law of Spirtness 4: Spiritual **+whirlwind+** energy is conserved between the past and the future. When the cycle is complete all spiritual energies are at zero, neither good nor bad.

SBTM/BTM/SV Postulate 5 Analysis: I believe that Remote Viewing can take place with thoughts and I believe that this is because the spirit can travel in the 5D, to another astral place, and that is reminiscent to a place on Earth. This is because of the Bible reading, that as above then so as below (Mat. VI:10 ABS, 1858). The universe has two levels, I think that this is possible because of Bosonic String Theory. In Bosonic String Theory there is the possibility for “26 dimensions,” (Ooguri & Yin, p.15). All of these dimensions do not need to be in the R3DT.

Law of Spirtness 5: The **+whirlwind+’s** circuit allows someone to use their spirit and tap into a psychic circuit to see all parts associated with the circuit using their third eye. [*, pp. 191-192]

Your spiritual body laying on sand, besides your physical body, in the dream realm looking at the Moon above, reflecting on the sea, while a UFO ball of light is approaching the two of you.

Appendix 3: Getting Your Computer to Have an Audio Editor

If you want to do SV then the easiest way I think would be to download an audio editor into your computer. I have an old desktop computer that I downloaded the Ubuntu Studio operating system that is based on Linux as a distro. There are some Linux enthusiast programmers that combine some great audio and video programs into a free computer operating system. I think that Linux is peer checked, so it is relatively safe to use, especially if you use this computer just for SV. Below are some steps to download it into your computer from my first book.

Installing the Ubuntu Studio operating system so you can have an audio editor on your computer.

You should have a flash USB drive that is at least 16GB in size, because you will use this to burn a bootable image of Ubuntu Studio onto it. The website is ubuntustudio.org and I will list the steps I took to do this below.

1) Assuming you have an Intel or AMD CPUs then download its latest version, Ubuntu Studio 22.04.2 LTS to your downloads folder. This should download one operating system in a *.iso file (the * is the exact filename) into your download folder with your internet browser, if not I know Chrome works well to do this. Otherwise, you will get an ark-folder and you might be able to

live install it from there. This might be helpful if you have a Microsoft Windows computer.

2) Next, launch Terminal or Konsole to navigate to the Downloads folder and check that the SHA256SUMS file matches the key when you input the command, sudo sha256sum *.iso to get the hash check which should be the same as the download website's hash check.
3) Apparently there is no way to be sure if you have a good *.iso unless you check the identification of the author in the keyring, in person through the procedure, outlined on the Ubuntu website.
4) Next make a *.iso image onto the USB drive with the commands:

    lsblk to find the name of your USB

drive, might be sdc, then:
sudo dd if=.iso of=/dev/sdc status="progress" bs=1M*

5) Next turn off the computer and boot to the USB drive by plugging-in the USB drive into a USB port, turn on the computer, and press the function key to get to the boot menu or just select to install the Linux system you wanted from the automated prompt.
6) I recommend choosing encryption, then your user name, password and select install.
7) After you log-in for the first time you should load Gufw, a firewall program, turn it on, and then load the software updates. [*, p.210]

Appendix 4: How I Did My 1040 Taxes After I Traded ES-Futures

I received a 1099-B because of my ES-futures trading. For the 2024 tax year I went to the irs.gov website to find information on where to file and what forms to use. I used the Form 8949, “Sales and Other Dispositions of Capital Assets” to record my “Costs” or my risk I put into my brokerage account and the “Gain or (loss)” for the year (from irs.gov). Form 8949 goes along with Schedule D for “Capital Gains and Losses” to complete the Form 1040. However, I might have done it wrong as my old tax preparer used Form 6781 “Gains and Losses From Section 1256 Contracts and Straddles.” The on-line IRS verified tax software did not have Form 6781 so I used Form 8949 instead.

I think that the cost basis is what you start out with and the ending amount is your profit or loss. For a profit, then the ending amount on the 1099-B would be a positive value, meaning that you now have more than the cost basis. The profit would be put onto Schedule D. IRS Form-6781 has a section for loss or a gain and my tax preparer took that number from my 1099-B and then needed to find the 40% and 60% of this number. So that the 40% is the "Short-term gain…." and it is used to go onto Schedule-D to calculate the carryover (loss), if any. Finally, the Schedule-D calculation went onto my Form-1040 for my income calculation.

Appendix 5: My Strategies I Thought of for Trading ES-Futures

There are ways you can trade ES-futures: as a novice you could look at the noise, as an experienced trader that always looses money by getting sloppy or as an expert trader that can get intuition for future movements and trade on that. The Professional Trader, I described, is the best trader because they can retire with money from trading. However, trading can go against you if you think the wrong thoughts.

If you see a trend and the market goes your way a little, then there is the fatal flaw that it will continue to go your way. The problem with this is that the market might have to retrace back to find new buyers and sellers. What happens with a retrace here is the trade looses all the money from the initial big movement, it just goes back. Alternatively, by using a stop and limit one can wait out the noise to see if the market is going in your trade's direction. This stop should reduce the amount of money lost as the market retraces back if the trade is making money.

The problem of waiting with a bad trade is to make a bigger stop. By making a bigger stop then the trader could loose more money, because it is a bad trade. The thought of the trader is to just wait it out, but they loose some or all of their money and they lock themselves into the trade to death. That is why the stop is important so that the stop is calculated to the situation of where the trader thinks the market is going. To then change this initial advice can mean the market changed. Maybe new sellers and buyers came in and the market dynamics changes without the trader knowing. If the trader loves the trade then they will want to make a bigger stop and hope their trade starts to go the right way, which never likely happens.

If you wait and watch for a big movement then this might be the time to see the rejection in the market and the chart will be showing a reversal in the market's direction or the market could continue to go lower. The trader needs to know when to enter into a trade because the market might go past their stop and push the trade out of the market. Everyone wants to find the bottom or top. Others will wait for the momentum to signal the change in direction and then get into the market as it is going the other way. These traders may not make as much money as the traders that want to just trade the bottom, but waiting just for the bottom is more risky.

A novice may think they can feel the market and just think it is going up or down and trade on that feeling. The problem here is that they could risk their whole trading account in risk to see if their vision happens. The novice here needs to come to a realization that the noise of the market finding its place doesn't always prove to correspond to larger moves like Fibonacci patterns repeating themselves.

The Fibonacci patterns can repeat, if you see them afterwards, but never the less the Fibonacci patterns do repeat. The repeating patterns hold because the ES-futures market is like a beast that is growing, staying the same or decreasing. An up pattern, as in a poke down and then curve up, in the same or larger time scales, can repeat so that being consistent of these Fibonacci patterns is an indicator of what the market can do or did, given no new news from a continuing output of news from the news media. How to see these patterns is with your intuition and then act on your familiar verified impulse with a safe trade in the market to see what happens.

It is better to trade using one's intuition so that a trend can be felt and then other signals in the chart can predict where the market is moving. If the market tries to go in a direction and has a big fail, where the market needs a big retrace, then waiting to find the bigger move might be less risky, if given a stop and limit is used too. The Fibonacci top might be known, but the bottom isn't. I'm going to try to predict the bottom with the Fibonacci tool, given the top is clear, and do this by matching the Fibonacci supports levels to what is already in the market. In this way the bottom could be predicted by using the Fibonacci tool. Using the Fibonacci tool is an Expert or Professional idea.

A novice probably could just buy or sell real quick when the ES-futures gets to a point level. An expert will know of a bourne, in at the support level or boundary, before it gets there. That might be one difference from the novice and expert, the expert will put a limit in, for a buy or short, while the novice will just trade in the market using more risk money. Why not wait till the market comes to you? That means you have to watch the market for it to come to you. Then on a conservative trade like this you will have more control of your risk money and be making a safer, more thoughtful, trade. The novice on the other hand, with the trade going bad will just wait, will be hoping that the trade goes in their direction. While the expert will be glad they didn't trade because the market is going the other way and they can safely reassess with a calm demeanor.

So rules that allow one to wait getting into the ES-futures market are superior to rules that allow going into any market condition. Even a nice run, on pages 262 to 268, shows how I made money then didn't make as much, then I could start losing money if I don't see this cycle. Take your time, my +Meself+ mentioned that God wanted me to only trade once a day, because it is accessing something deep, and this requires only once because it is powerful, like faith. **~Behavior is key to trading Matthew.~** In a separate SV I found: **~If you want to get enlightened you can do that with good behavior.~**

Appendix 6: My thoughts on how to manifest your destiny.

When you put your consciousness to the test then you will see that psychic forces can attack it. Psychic vampirism can spiritually go into your mind and change your viewpoint. This is subconscious and there is no way to know this unless you enter the subconscious. This is why you need to do SV.

If we can understand that the ecosystem of spirit is apparent when we listen to SV, then we can find ways to prevent these forces to take control of ourselves. There is a keystone spirit and you could guess, it's +Say-tin+ and we know if this keystone falls then the other evil spirits around +Say-tin+ also fall.

This is like in the Garden of Eden where the apple tree was a keystone fruit and when it was disturbed then Adam and Eve fell to Earth. Let's try to be better and know that spirit can feed on spirit and the body is flesh that can sin. The body sins when it attacks the mind or consciousness. If the consciousness is attacked then we might loose our mind and fall into death, like sin will always do to us.

I think the answer to this problem of sin is to follow the Ten Commandments and attempt to get manna from the spirit. If spirit is in a food web then that means the consciousness could consume some spirit to provide for the body. If we sin then the body will consume the consciousness. So we must think better thoughts before and change our behavior to lead a spiritual life, making our body aligned with our higher self, the +meself+ so we can see the subconscious and remember our dreams so we can interpret those dreams and manifest the life we want to live.

In the last book of the Bible there is the white stone given to the prophet (Rev. II:17 ABS, 1858). So I say (not taking away from The Revelation in the Bible) is to use your ears, do SV, get meat from the spirit realm, receive a white stone from your +meself+ so that you can get a name and that no one else knows it. Use this gift to help others. That is what I'm doing with this book, is to help others, to be successful and live in a better neighborhood.

References

American Bible Society. (1858). *The Holy Bible : containing the Old and New Testaments* [DX Reader versions]. Retrieved from https://archive.org/details/holybiblecontain00amer_4/page/n8/mode/1up

Mandell, M. (November 12, 2024). *How to Trade ES-Futures.* LaVergne, TN: Independently published. ISBN: 979-8-9919098-0-8.

Mandell, M. (October 30, 2024). *2intone dot us,* Edition: 2. Monee, IL: Independently published. ISBN: 979-8-3408695-7-9.

Ooguri, H., & Yin, Z. (1997). *TASI Lectures on Perturbative String Theories. arXIV: High Energy Physics – Theory (1996): n. Pag.* Retrieved from https://arxiv.org/abs/hep-th/9612254

Index